South Kensington Museum

The South Kensington Museum

examples of the works of art in the museum and of the decorations of the building

with brief descriptions

South Kensington Museum

The South Kensington Museum
examples of the works of art in the museum and of the decorations of the building with brief descriptions

ISBN/EAN: 9783337853143

Printed in Europe, USA, Canada, Australia, Japan

Cover: Foto ©Andreas Hilbeck / pixelio.de

More available books at **www.hansebooks.com**

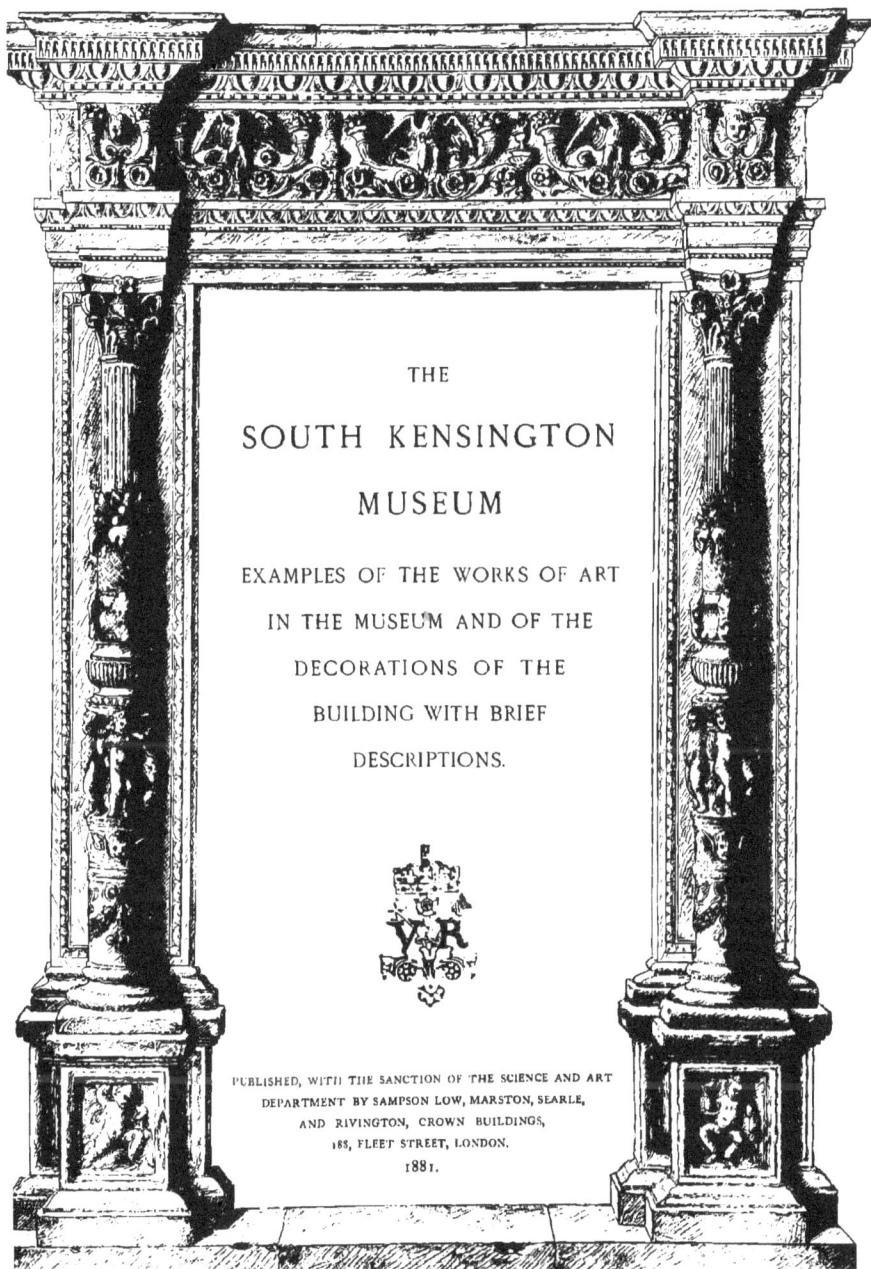

THE

SOUTH KENSINGTON

MUSEUM

EXAMPLES OF THE WORKS OF ART

IN THE MUSEUM AND OF THE

DECORATIONS OF THE

BUILDING WITH BRIEF

DESCRIPTIONS.

PUBLISHED, WITH THE SANCTION OF THE SCIENCE AND ART
DEPARTMENT BY SAMPSON LOW, MARSTON, SEARLE,
AND RIVINGTON, CROWN BUILDINGS,
188, FLEET STREET, LONDON.
1881.

THE present volume contains representations of nearly eighty specimens of works of art, selected from the collections in the South Kensington Museum. These are printed from etchings which have been made by the students—past and present—in training as Art teachers, in the etching class at the South Kensington Art schools since about the year 1865, under the direction, first, of the late Richard J. Lane, A.R.A., then of T. O. Barlow, A.R.A., and now of Mr. A. Legros.

Besides these etchings illustrations are given of portions of the buildings and decorations, several of which have been engraved on wood.

The chief object aimed at by the Department of Science and Art in this publication has been to put within the reach of art-students and workmen useful or suggestive examples of design and workmanship, at the lowest possible price. An adaptation of lithography has enabled the publishers to meet the views of the Department.

Some of the works of art which are engraved in this volume are of the highest excellence; such, for instance, as the silver mounting of the agate cup, No. 63. Another specimen of English silver work equally good is interesting and historically important, as showing the estimation in which Chinese porcelain was held in England so far back as the reign of queen Elizabeth. Other examples have been selected from ancient and mediæval works in ivory (especially the famous leaf of the Roman diptych of the second century, No. 23), from chests and cabinets in wood, from Italian bronzes of the fifteenth and sixteenth centuries, and from ecclesiastical metal work of the middle ages. With reference to this last, the brief remarks made in the description of the silver pyx, No. 74, will explain the reason why so large a proportion of works of art from the tenth to the sixteenth century is supplied by what has been preserved in the treasuries of churches and monasteries.

A few art objects have been included not so much as excellent and valuable in themselves but as likely to give hints to workmen in more respects than one. For instance, the brass plaque, No. 22, and the covers of the ivory writing tablets, No. 75

One very celebrated piece of Japanese work in iron is engraved, No. 40.

CONTENTS.

CONTENTS.

CONTENTS.

CONTENTS.

With the Sanction of the
of the Committee of

Science and Art Department
Council on Education.

IN MONTHLY PARTS, EACH CONTAINING EIGHT PLATES, WITH
DESCRIPTIONS, FOR ONE SHILLING.

THE

SOUTH KENSINGTON
MUSEUM.

IN order to render the Art-Treasures of South Kensington available for
the instruction of all classes, it is proposed to publish a series of
etchings and engravings of many of the most important objects in the
Museum, *at the lowest possible price.*

Taking advantage of the many new processes for the reproduction of
drawings and objects of art, each monthly part of "THE SOUTH KEN-
SINGTON MUSEUM" will contain eight pages of illustrations, with descriptions, for the price of one shilling; and for the especial benefit of students,
arrangements have been made for the sale of single plates at the book-
stall of the Museum at *one penny* or *twopence each.*

In this series will be included representations of DECORATIVE ART of all countries and all times, from objects in the South Kensington Museum under the following classes :—

> SCULPTURE : Works in Marble, Stone, Terra-Cotta, and other Materials.
> BRONZES: Statuettes, Medallions, Plaques, Coins.
> DECORATIVE PAINTING.
> DECORATIVE FURNITURE and CARVED WOOD-WORK.
> CARVED IVORY-WORK and BONE.
> ECCLESIASTICAL METAL-WORK.
> GOLD and SILVERSMITH'S WORK.
> JEWELLERY and BIJOUTERIE.
> DECORATIVE METAL-WORK.
> ENAMELS : Oriental and Limoges.
> POTTERY OF ALL COUNTRIES.
> GLASS : Oriental, Venetian, and German.
> DECORATIVE BOOKBINDING.
> TEXTILE FABRICS : Embroidery and Lace.
> DECORATIVE CLOCKS and WATCHES.
> ORNAMENTAL CUTLERY.
> ORIGINAL DESIGNS for Works of Decorative Art.

The plates will be carefully printed with a Japanese tint on thick plate paper, atlas 8vo., and will be included in a stout wrapper, ornamented with a drawing of "the Genoa Doorway," recently acquired by the Museum.

Crown Buildings, 188, *Fleet Street.*

WEST STAIRCASE

M R. W. F. MOODY designed the decorations of this staircase, of which the first flight is shown in the etching. The ornamentation of the walls is carried out in enamelled terra-cotta, the colours being white, buff, and celadon green : executed by Minton and Co. The ceiling, dome, the panels above the dado, and the spandrels, are in Mr. Colin Minton Campbell's new process of vitrified ceramic painting.

In the two painted glass windows seen on the first landing are figures (designed by Mr. Moody and executed by Messrs. Powell) of men who are celebrated either in science or in art.

PANEL IN WINDOW RECESS.
SOUTH KENSINGTON MUSEUM.
Designed by Godfrey Sykes.

I. 1

WEST STAIRCASE, LEADING TO THE CERAMIC GALLERY.
South Kensington Museum.

CRUET.

CRYSTAL AND SILVER GILT.

No. 15—1864.

A VERY fine example, believed to be French work of the fifteenth century. Possibly we are right in thus attributing it : but there is
nothing so absolutely distinct as to prevent the supposition that it may be
English. The upright straps which secure the wide rim surrounding the
neck of the crystal to the foot or base have a decided English character,
which is commonly found in cups and jugs similarly mounted about a
hundred years later. The same may be said of the small beaded ornament following the mouldings of the cusped lobes at the foot.

The crystal vase itself is probably much older even than the mount;
and the cruet itself may have been one of a pair used at mass in some
catholic church ; the one for wine, the other for water. The body of the
vase is round, with slightly expressed divisions or flat flutings; the handle is
flat at the top, bending downwards at an acute angle. A rib or collar is
left a little below the neck, over which the upright bands (before spoken of)
are bent. The crystal cover is a half globe or circle.

The mount, silver gilt, is very rich ; and consists of a foot, a wide neck
from which the spout issues, a handle, and decorations of the cover. The
handle is (as it were) independent of the crystal handle, and is fixed above
it, as if to be used by a second finger; it is partly enamelled. The upper
part of the neck is polygonal, chased with cusped arches each finished below
with a fleur-de-lys. The use of this emblem is the chief ground for supposing
the work to be French ; by no means leaving it beyond doubt, as the lily
was a common emblem in the decoration of church utensils attached to
altars or chapels dedicated to the blessed Virgin. Below the line of the
fleur-de-lys, and divided from it by a moulding of small beads, is a rich
architectural arcade. The top edge is ornamented with similar lines and a
zigzag moulding ending in two graceful volutes with acorn eyes, which
form a purchase by which to raise the lid. The spout is a short tube
issuing from a lion's head. A tall finial, with very elegantly designed
leaves, surmounts the crystal cover.

The foot is somewhat flat, spreading in six round lobes, each chased
with cuspings and fleurs-de-lys and below them is a beaded moulding. The
height of the cruet is about eight inches and a half.

Bought for 120*l.*

I. 2

CREDENCE, OR SIDEBOARD.

CARVED OAK.

No. 8439—1863.

IT is not certain to what country we can attribute this fine piece of furniture: but it is most probably Flemish. Whether in England, France, or Flanders, the fourteenth and fifteenth centuries produced artists in wood who were quite equal, both for design and for the quality of their work, to those who have left us the churches and other buildings of that time. The general character of all wood-work, and therefore of furniture, partook of an architectural type. Coffers and chests, panelling in rooms, stall ends in churches, bench ends in halls and rooms, were commonly designed after the patterns of tracery of doors and windows. Little buttresses and pinnacles were placed on the angles and divisions between the panels.

The sideboard engraved is an excellent example of this kind of work, now very rarely found complete. It was formerly in the celebrated Soulages collection. The date given in the etching is too early by some fifty or sixty years: the style shows it to be of the end rather than the beginning of the fifteenth century. The arches are all very flat or circular, and there is a mixture of styles in the angle buttresses which we see in the old Bishop's palace at Liege, in the Exchange at Antwerp, and in other monuments of the civil architecture of that period in Belgium.

The centre projects from its base with a narrowed front and canted sides. These are divided from the square part at the back and from the front by elegant buttresses of about one inch and a half projection. The panels are cut into rounded arches and are in two tiers. In the upper row are single figures of the cardinal virtues, with bas-reliefs of St. Catharine of Alexandria and St. Barbara in smaller arched panels on each side of the door. The iron hinge straps form two narrow panels, and are richly decorated with pierced tracery work and three heads in relief. Below these

I. 3

upper tiers is a lower tier with reliefs representing Fortitude, Cowardice, Temperance, Excess, &c. The door in the centre is separated from a narrow panel on each side by two projecting beak-headed grotesques. The buttress legs are joined by frame pieces cut into wide and narrow arches on the front and sides respectively; a horizontal bar connects them at the feet. The square side panels are also carved. The upper shelf is hollow, has round arches at each end with short pinnacle columns at the corners, and probably had, originally, a depressed round arch in front. The place of this is now supplied by a horizontal panel of cinquecento arabesque with the arms of De Clare on a shield in the middle. The same bearings (or three chevrons gules) may, however, have been those of some continental owner in the sixteenth century.

The cabinet stands about 5 feet 3 inches in height, by 2 feet 1 inch in width.

Bought for 8ol.

CREDENCE IN CARVED OAK. FRENCH, EARLY 15th CENT.
H. 5 FT 3/6 IN.; W. 4 FT 4 IN.; D. 2 FT. 6 IN. (SOULAGES COLL.) S.K.M. (7842.49).
F.A. S.U.G. PHOTO. LITH. CO.

BOWL OR BOX.

BELL-METAL.

No. 2812—1856.

BRONZE is obtained from the melting together in certain proportions two metals, copper and tin ; and the mixed substance not only differs in colour from either of its constituent elements, but in various other qualities. As regards colour, for example, in place of the white of the one and the ruby of the other we have a golden brown. Bronze varies in quality according to the quantities used of the two metals, and many experiments have been made, in the way of analysis and otherwise, to ascertain the proportions from which the fine antique bronze was produced. The famous *Æs Corinthiacum*, Corinthian bronze, is supposed to have had small additions of other metals, gold and silver ; but the story on which this tradition rests has but slight foundation. Eighty-eight parts of copper to twelve of tin may be taken as the general result of many analyses of ancient bronzes. In later time, since the sixteenth century, other metals are also employed, such as lead or brass ; but in very small quantities. Bell-metal is a variety of bronze, with a somewhat larger proportion of tin, and the addition of silver, according to some manufacturers, in order to improve the sound. Instructions to make bell-metal in the twelfth century prescribe a fifth part to be of tin.

This bowl was probably made about the year 1600, and may have been intended for a tobacco box. The workmanship is Flemish, and the design of the decoration, which is in low relief, is good and elegant. It consists of foliated scroll-work, running round both the box and the cover, divided by masks and other ornaments. Some very excellent artists in bronze worked in the Netherlands and in Holland about the beginning of the seventeenth century, such as Adrian Fries ; and we may add Fiammingo, who supplied several designs.

Bought for 4l. 16s.

I. 4

JUG.

PORCELAIN, SILVER GILT MOUNTING.

No. 7915—1862.

ONE of the most important and remarkable objects in the Museum. Not because of the rarity of the jug itself, nor of the especial goodness of the mounting, but because the two are combined. Pieces of porcelain are in the collection quite as good in quality, and examples no less beautiful of Elizabethan silver work. But the jug is mounted upon a piece of plate bearing the hall mark of 1585.

It is quite possible that the jug may be much older than even the end of the sixteenth century; but it cannot be of later date. No history is attached to it, and one can only guess how it came to England; whether direct from China, or through some earlier possessor in Italy or France. That the first English owner set a high and just value on his acquisition is quite evident from the care and money which he spent upon it.

The porcelain is like the famous blue and white Nankin : octagonal in shape; and the upright spout is connected with the body by a scroll of porcelain. The handle is of the usual form; and the body is decorated with small figures of men or boys, one in each panel, divided by upright ribs. The mounts and cover are of the best character of Elizabethan work of that period; boldly embossed with fruit and flowers.

There is at this time (1880) on loan at Bethnal Green a cup (if we may call it so) in the exact form and shape of a modern teapot, also with a fine English mount, but not hall marked : not later than about 1610.

This jug stands 10 inches in height.

Bought for 75l.

TEA POT ORIENTAL PORCELAIN WHITE & BLUE MOUNTED SILVER
AND WORK HOLE S.K.M. V.9.5. 2 PRITCHARD HST

15

MIRROR CASE.

IVORY.

No. 1617—1855.

THERE are several good examples of mediæval ivory mirror cases in the Museum, and this is one of the finest. Probably of French art, it may possibly, nevertheless, be attributed without rashness to an English sculptor. The date is of the best period of the fourteenth century.

The mirror cases of the middle ages were either in two parts, almost always round, which screwed or fitted closely one within the other, forming a front and cover: or they were made of a single piece of ivory or wood, &c. (as the material might be), with a hollow cut out at the back for the glass or metal which formed the mirror. It is not known when glass was introduced instead of the earlier metallic mirror: very probably about the year 1200.

Ladies using mirrors at their toilets frequently are to be met with in illuminations of manuscripts of the fourteenth and fifteenth centuries, and generally in the shape and size which we find in the ivories which have come down to our own times. Ivory was always a very expensive material, and therefore was usually highly ornamented also. The most frequent subjects which the artist sculptured were taken, as with combs, caskets, and writing-tablets, from the popular romances and ballads of the time. Among them, especially, from the famous "Romance of the Rose" and the "Siege of the Castle of Love."

The attack and surrender of the "Castle of Love" supplies the subject which decorates the present example. In front and occupying the centre is the closed gateway, but with raised portcullis. A tower flanks the entrance on each side, and behind it is the battlemented wall, over which the ladies have been watching and attempting to defend themselves against the assault.

On the left at the top of a rope ladder a knight, from whose head the

I. 6

helmet has been removed, has just reached the parapet where he is helped over by one of the ladies. Close behind him, on horseback, is another knight, who raises his sword with one hand by the point, and with the other lifts the heavy helmet from his head. Inside the battlements in the middle, a knight already received into the castle, probably the chief, kisses and embraces one of the ladies; and by their side other knights are making their way over the wall: one of them, the easier to get up, stands on the pommel of the saddle of his horse. He is further helped by another knight on horseback who half pushes him over.

Above this part of the castle is a square tower with a balcony ornamented with trefoils in open or pierced work. In this an allegorical figure of Love stands, winged like a seraph and striking with an arrow in each hand two ladies. Two other ladies sit at the ends of the balcony looking over, as if still watching or meditating. Three lions, carved with much vigour, creep round the outside rim of the mirror case. A fourth has been broken off. The diameter of the case is about five inches and a half.

The workmanship displayed upon this beautiful mirror case is quite equal to the design; and it has been well and carefully preserved, the only injury being the loss of one lion. It is also worthy of special study and examination, as furnishing an excellent illustration of this particular portion of the history of the siege, in which at last the defenders of the castle surrender it. The attack is an equally frequent subject; where the ladies resist the knights by throwing down on them showers of roses.

Bought for 50*l.* 12*s.*

DESIGN FOR A NICHE.

No. 2235.   Art Library.

A PEN and bistre tint drawing upon paper, ascribed to Pierino del
Vaga.   Richly decorated pilasters are on the sides of the niche, and
above it two nearly nude sitting figures are placed in front of the pediment,
between whom is a cartouche, intended probably for a coat of arms.

Pierino del Vaga was born in a village near Florence about the year
1500, and after studying as a pupil of Ridolfo Ghirlandaio, went to Rome,
where he was employed by Raffaelle in the execution of his designs for the
Loggie of the Vatican.   He died in 1547.

DESIGN FOR A NICHE.
From an original drawing ascribed to Pierino del Vaga.
In the Art Library, South Kensington Museum.

17

APELLES.

GLASS MOSAIC.

THIS etching is from the original cartoon by Mr. E. J. Poynter, R.A., which has been executed in Italian glass mosaic by Salviati of Venice. The portrait forms one of the series of eminent painters, sculptors, and architects, filling the panels in the arcade of the upper part of the central or loan Court.

Apelles died about B.C. 340.

PANEL OF WINDOW-FRAME.
SOUTH KENSINGTON MUSEUM.
Designed by Godfrey Sykes.

E.J POYNTER RA PINX   BERNARD CCOLLIER SC

APELLES

1 8.

ITALIAN

MIRROR FRAME.

WALNUT WOOD.

No. 7695—1861.

THE mirror itself is metal: and the frame belongs to the best period of Italian wood carving, when the treatment of classical details in architecture and wood-work was still new, and was managed with an amount of care that was lost when the study of Roman classicalism led to the adoption of vast proportions in structure, and consequent coarseness in the decoration required. The work cannot be put later than the very beginning of the sixteenth century; that is, before the year 1520. Mirrors of so large a size as this were always of metal in the middle ages: although glass undoubtedly was used as far back as the fourteenth century for the small round hand mirrors. The present example was purchased with the Soulages collection.

The mirror stands upon a square base with canted angles, shaped like the stem of a chalice or drinking cup. The four large sides rise to within three inches of the frame, gradually diminishing so as to contain four slightly concave panels, which are decorated with carved emblems, each in a circle. The intervening narrow panels on the angles have palmette work, which also runs round the base. Below, is a straight plinth with upper and lower bead mouldings, raising the decorated border on a sort of stand.

The emblems in the four panels are—1. An elephant, the meaning of which is not very clear: but may possibly have reference to some story or tradition in the family of the lady for whom the mirror was intended. 2. A goose carrying a pin in its mouth; an allusion, some say, to the classic notions of the fidelity of that fowl. 3. A civet cat, prized for its musk perfume. 4. A knot of twisted hair, fastened at the bottom to a base of velvet or other material for a head dress.

The mirror is set upon this stand; but between the two is an interval

I. 9

of about three inches, and this portion is worked into a wide and well shaped baluster with a knop and collars turned in the lathe. By this the mirror was easily held up for use; the knop giving a firm hold for the hand. Small square tablets are placed immediately under and in the middle of the square frame, having on each side scrolls which serve as the main supports. These scrolls and a similar tablet are repeated at the top of the frame. The little tablets have carved on them the device of a small mound with three "Marguerites" or daisies. The frame itself is ornamented with delicate line mouldings formed of notches, plait work, guilloches, &c: with a broad band of palmette leaves outside. These leaves and all the other details are modelled and relieved with great delicacy; and the same tender and beautiful treatment, carried out with most careful and excellent workmanship, is evident in every part.

This mirror, upon which no pains nor expense was spared, must have been made for some lady in high position; and the daisies carved upon the little panels suggest that possibly she was Marguerite of Valois, daughter of Charles of Orleans and Louise of Savoy. She was born in 1492; was first married in 1509, and, by her second marriage in 1526 to the king of Navarre, became the mother of Henry the fourth, king of France. She died in 1549.

The frame stands in height 2 feet 7 inches: the plate of metal is 10¼ inches by a little less than 9 inches.

Bought for 150*l.*

SILVER PARCEL-GILT TAZZA   DUTCH OR GERMAN

CUP.

SILVER, PARCEL GILT.

No. 320—1854.

GERMAN work of the seventeenth century, and useful as an example of the general style and manner of that period and country. The bowl is a segment of a somewhat flattened globe, with the upper part of the outside in plain metal. The stem, which is the best designed part of the cup, has a central knop formed by four curling scrolls alternating with four light flowers. A crown of light flat flower-work, falling over in flowers and leaves, covers the point of junction between the stem and the bowl. The foot spreads below a short circular pedestal, and is decorated with arabesques and strap-work.

The inside of the bowl is beaten up with a composition of figures: Tobit carrying a fish, accompanied by his dog and the archangel, in a landscape.

The design of this cup is better than the execution; on the whole, the piece is effective in outline and arrangement, and the fine beaten leaf-work round the junction of the stem and bowl is light and graceful.

The cup stands rather more than 6 inches in height.

Bought for 15l.

BRONZE KNOCKER, ITALIAN, ABOUT 1500 H.IL.IN.
W.13 IN SOULAGES COLL S.K.M (Nº 373·85)

M.SULLIVAN FECIT

KNOCKER.

No. 573—1865.

A SUPERB example, Italian work of the sixteenth century, which was formerly in the Soulages collection. In the lower part two mermaids or syrens are embracing. On the shoulder of one of these an amorino stands, filling the centre of the group; and on either side is an undraped boy.

Some have attributed this knocker to John of Bologna; nor is it unworthy of so great an artist. Few finer specimens exist of highly artistic modelling as applied to objects of every-day use. Still fewer can be seen upon the doors of the palaces for which they were designed: originally, in pairs.

Another knocker in the Museum, No. 588 '53, may be compared with this. In point of design this last may be praised the most; but in both of them the execution is equally admirable and masterly.

Bought for 8ol.

.

THE HEAD OF A PASTORAL STAFF.

IVORY.

No. 218—1865.

IT is more difficult to decide upon the country where this remarkable crosier-head was made, than upon the date of it. Generally supposed to be of German origin, it may with equal probability be ascribed to an English artist. The character, in some details, of the draperies and their ornaments is not unlike the style of carvings in ivory of that school, and the same date—the twelfth century.

The outside of the volute is carved in high relief, with many small figures. Some of these, issuing (as it were) from the body of the ivory itself, show a treatment which is almost if not quite unique. The subjects are not all easy of explanation.

There is no doubt as to the meaning of the sculpture at the base—namely, the Nativity: the blessed Virgin draws aside curtains and contemplates the Infant in His cradle. Her robe is open at the throat, with an ornamental border. Above this, the Virgin is seen again, seated, and suckling the Child. St. Joseph, close by, stretches out his hands to Him. On the top of the volute three women lie, sleeping; immediately below, on the slope of the volute, reclines a half clothed figure, which a man, standing under, appears ready to receive: this man is assisted by a woman on the other side, not shown in the etching. It is difficult even to guess at what these figures are meant to represent.

The extremity of the volute is formed by an angel with extended arms supporting a small lamb resting before a cross. On the reverse is the Virgin asleep; and the Infant above lying in swaddling clothes.

Bought for 140*l.*

CRUCIFIX.

SILVER GILT.

No. 181—1866.

PERHAPS German work, early in the fifteenth century; and more richly decorated than crucifixes either at that period or later are generally found. The figure of our Saviour is on a scale considerably less than usual, but this is accounted for by the small space left for the extended arms upon the cross-beam.

The four limbs of the cross end in large quatrefoils, having on their edges a moulding of small grains. Each contains a symbol of the four evangelists and a scroll with the name. The stem immediately under the lowest quatrefoil is surrounded on the front and back with a rich arcade of arches on either side. These arches are headed by crocketed gables with trefoil cuspings of tracery. Six figures stand under the arches, and tiny buttresses dividing the sides from the front and back serve also to support the corners of the canopy. The figures represent the blessed Virgin, St. John, St. Mary Magdalen, St. Bartholomew, and two other saints; one of these last is a female saint, and each of them holds a palm branch.

The base is plain, spreading somewhat flatly but with good effect into six lobes; beneath which is an upright border with a very pretty diamond-traced ornament. The base has also two small shields; one coat bears, argent, a fess gules, over all a tree with three leaves, rooted proper; the other, argent, an escutcheon sable.

The head of our Lord leans towards the left side, in death. The body is but slightly clothed, having a wide-folded cincture round the loins. Each hand extends towards a tallow-cut sapphire, and a small facetted sapphire is set over the head. The title INRI is in Gothic letters upon a scroll, of which the ends pass beyond the width of the upright of the cross. The whole figure of our Lord is very carefully wrought.

The back of the crucifix is plain, with an opening in the centre for relics. Inside there remains a small cross of crystal, split and hollowed in the middle, and fastened along the two sides by a wire sewing. The ends of the wire are still secured by the old official seal of authentication, but the relics seem, nevertheless, to have been removed.

There are several similar crucifixes, and of about the same date, in the Museum, with which the present example may be very profitably compared ; for instance, a gilt copper cross, with a parcel gilt silver figure, No. 1172' 64. In this, again, the figure is small in proportion, and without the same necessity, because of want of room. The base is of the same style, but even more plain and simple, and there is also a cavity behind for relics.

The remarkable feature in the crucifix here engraved, namely, the architectural arcade and figures of saints, is much more commonly found in chalices or monstrances.

This crucifix stands about 10 inches high.

Bought for 10*l.*

DESIGN FOR END OF PRINCE CONSORT GALLERY.

In the South Kensington Museum.

A DESIGN.

BY THE LATE GODFREY SYKES.

THIS design has not yet been fully carried out. It was intended for the end of the gallery in the Museum in which some of the finest examples of gold and silversmith's work, enamels, and metal-work of various kinds are now placed. The gallery gives access to the singing balcony brought from the church of Santa Maria at Florence, from which the northern court of the Museum, now chiefly filled with mediæval and renaissance Italian marbles and reproductions, is overlooked.

The doorway itself is finished ; but not the double arch nor the decorations of the pilasters. These are still wanting. The medallion portrait of the Prince Consort and the figures on each side have been executed in ceramic mosaic by Minton, Hollins & Co. The date 1857 is the year in which the buildings at South Kensington were first opened.

The late Mr. Godfrey Sykes died in his forty-first year, in 1866 : and if he had lived would have been a very distinguished man. He received his first education in art as a pupil in the government School of Art at Sheffield, in which he was afterwards a master. A great spur was given to his exertions, and a way opened to thought and aspiration, by a journey which he made to Italy. He had in himself a germ of real power in design and a keen perception of natural beauty. The capacity of designing correctly is less uncommon than the sense of the right application of this capacity to decoration. Ordinary training may enable an artist to model a figure or a vegetable rightly, but it will not impart the knowledge of the great restraint required in applying this skill to decoration. Here the golden rule is to know how to suppress details, where to stop, what to emphasize, or what to omit. These rare qualities were possessed by Mr. Sykes, and we need no further proof than his first great work, the arcades of the Horticultural Gardens ; especially of the conservatory. The capitals, the columns, the circular panels and many other details, prove that he was not only endowed with great power of design, but with, what is so rare in our time, a just feeling of the decorative treatment needed to secure a true effect.

The work chiefly aimed at by Godfrey Sykes was decorative, and the buildings at South Kensington, for which the larger portion of the drawings which he left behind him was intended, are as yet not completed. A few years hence the extent and importance of these works will be justly recognized and widely appreciated.

SinF LEIGHTON P.R.A Pinx   B COLLIER Sc

CIMABUE

GIOVANNI CIMABUE.

CERAMIC MOSAIC.

THE original cartoon from which this etching is taken was painted about fourteen years ago by Sir Frederick Leighton, now president of the Royal Academy. It has been reproduced in ceramic mosaic by Messrs. Minton and Co. as one of the series of portraits filling the panels in the arcade of the upper part of the central or loan Court.

Cimabue was born in Florence in 1240. His first celebrated picture, a Madonna and Child, was painted for the church of S. Maria Novella in that city, where it is still preserved. It is said to have been the largest altar-piece produced up to that date, and was carried in festive procession from his house outside the walls of the city to the church.

An early painting by Sir Frederick Leighton representing this procession, now the property of the Queen, is well known.

Cimabue died about 1302.

PANEL IN BALCONY OF QUADRANGLE, SOUTH KENSINGTON MUSEUM.
Designed by Godfrey Sykes.

BAS-RELIEF:

ON THE FRONT OF A SARCOPHAGUS.

No. 75—1879.

THE collection in the South Kensington Museum of Italian mediæval works in marble and terra-cotta is unequalled by any other similar collection either in this or any foreign country. Gathered together at its commencement in 1857, under the advice and with the approval of Mr. J. C. Robinson, at that time curator of the Museum, it contains many most admirable examples, and among them none which exceeds in beauty of design or excellence of workmanship the bas-relief which is here engraved. No engraving—no photograph, even—can justly express the qualities of the original : it must, in truth, be seen in order to be fully appreciated. For this superb marble the nation is also indebted to the kindness and energy of Mr. Robinson, who, as soon as he heard of its existence, lost no time in securing it for the Museum.

A brief description cannot be given in better words than those in which Mr. Robinson himself wrote of the bas-relief in a letter published about May, 1879. He says: " This is a marble sarcophagus, hollowed out and large enough to contain a dead body ; in front is the exquisitely sculptured presentment of the personage whose relics doubtless it once enshrined, and at each end is a draped boy angel, swinging a censer. Nothing finer can be conceived than this exquisite recumbent figure, sculptured in the lowest relief—rather, as it were, painted in marble than carved. Clad from head to foot in a diaphanous veil or shroud, a crown upon her head, which is surrounded by a nimbus, the holy maiden is not dead, but sleeping as if in a trance of eternal beatitude. Intensely human, but divinely beautiful, the work is a triumph of the world's highest art."

The previous history of the sarcophagus, so far as it is known, is thus

I. 16

given by Mr. Robinson : " The recent owner purchased it at Padua, where, in a garden or vineyard, it had probably for a century or two done duty as a water-trough, the sculptured face placed downwards, so that the very existence of the figure had in consequence been forgotten. It needed no special acuteness to divine the train of circumstances which might have led to this ignoble misappropriation. There was a time in Italy (in the seventeenth century) when the debased taste of the age gave rise to a mania for the so-called restoration and reconstruction of ecclesiastical monuments, and on all hands the beautiful sculptured altars and other great works of the period of the revival were voted old-fashioned and barbarous. Hundreds of noble works of art were then ruthlessly swept away and replaced by overcharged structures of gilded wood and metal, coloured marbles, and mosaics—rich in everything but art. Although the strongly-marked individual manner of Donatello was stamped in every line and form of the work in question, so that there could be no uncertainty as to the authorship, the fact of its having come to light at Padua was an additional evidence ; for it is well known that Donatello found for many years a home in that city, and there executed a vast number of works. He seems to have returned to Florence shortly before the year 1456 ; the sarcophagus, therefore, must have been executed prior to that date.

" There was a local saint of Padua—Santa Justina—and her relics were enclosed in a shrine or chest under the high altar of the church dedicated to her in that city, but when the choir was rebuilt in 1627 the relics were translated into a sumptuous vault under the new altar. This Santa Justina was a king's daughter, and it will be noted that the effigy wears a regal crown as well as a nimbus."

We may conclude it to be almost certain, therefore, that this sarcophagus was designed and made by Donatello in order to receive the relics of Saint Justina.

Donatello was born in 1383, and died in 1466.

The sarcophagus is 2 feet 2 inches in height, 6 feet 5½ inches long, and 18½ inches wide.

Bought for 186l.

Santa Maria, Pisa

17.

CENTRAL RECESS

IN THE PRINCIPAL QUADRANGLE.

AN external view of the windows in a recess which gives light to the ceramic gallery near the stairs leading to the lecture theatre. This portion of the building was built from designs by the late Captain Fowke, R.E.

The terra cotta columns supporting the arcade were designed by Godfrey Sykes and executed by Blanchard and Co. They are fifteen feet in height. Each column consists of six drums, three of which are fluted and surrounded by branches of trees or boughs, modelled from nature and laid over the flutings. The alternate drums have figure subjects, typifying the three ages of man; childhood, manhood, and old age. Childhood has, 1, the baby; 2, playfellows; 3, playing at soldiers. Manhood: 1, the bridegroom; 2, the warrior; 3, ambition; 4, the cup of temptation. Old age: 1, the dignity of age; 2, the weariness; 3, the helplessness.

The three drums are placed in the different columns so as to present different sides to the spectator, thus ensuring also great variety.

G.SYKES. INV.

PANEL IN TERRA COTTA, DESIGNED BY GODFREY SYKES.

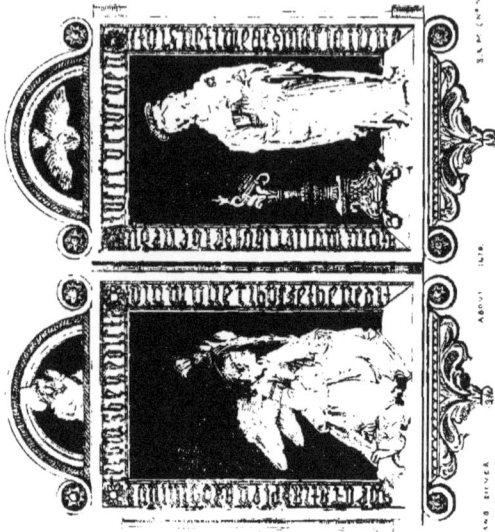

DIPTYCH.

GILT BRONZE AND SILVER, WITH FIGURES IN BONE.

No. 4355—1857.

DIPTYCHS, or folding tablets for devotional purposes, of this character are extremely rare. The present beautiful example is Italian, of the middle of the fifteenth century. Each tablet is surrounded with a square border, carrying an inscription; and above each is a decorated tympanum. On each tablet is a single figure, carved in bone; and placed upon a background of black horn.

The subject is the Annunciation. Upon the left tablet the archangel kneels upon one knee, having his right arm thrown with a gesture of reverence across his breast and holding a blooming lily in the left hand. Round his head is a coronet of flowers, and he is vested in a long robe doubled at the girdle. The right foot is shown bare. The figure is admirably designed and well executed: both the attitude and the expression are full of humility and devotion. Upon the other leaf is represented the blessed Virgin; standing, and clothed as usual in a gown or tunic with a very ample pall or cloak. On her left shoulder is a small flower or leaf. Her head is covered with a light veil, above which is a nimbus. She, also, stands in an attitude of humility and obedience, one hand crossing her breast and with eyes cast down. Before the Virgin a tall reading-desk is placed: having on it an open book to which a cloth is attached, as was common in the middle ages, to protect the binding. This desk is carefully modelled after those used in Italy about 1490, the early renaissance period.

In the left tympanum is a half-figure representing God the Father holding up the right hand in the act of benediction. In the right the Sacred Dove is descending upon the Virgin's head.

Round the border is a legend in large square letters (silver upon a gilt ground), which begins round the half containing the archangel. After the 𝕬𝖛𝖊 𝕸𝖆𝖗𝖎𝖆 is added " 𝕹𝖊 𝖙𝖎𝖒𝖊𝖆𝖘 𝕸𝖆𝖗𝖎𝖆, 𝖎𝖓𝖛𝖊𝖓𝖎𝖘𝖙𝖎 𝖌𝖗𝖆𝖙𝖎𝖆𝖒." The out-

I. 18

side of the diptych is formed of two smaller panels of silver, each containing a candelabrum ornament, gilt : round this is a border of niello. There is also another legend, continued through the two leaves, " 𝕾𝖆𝖑𝖛𝖊 𝖗𝖆𝖉𝖎𝖗 𝖘𝖆𝖓𝖈𝖙𝖆 𝖊𝖗 𝖖𝖚𝖆 𝖒𝖚𝖓𝖉𝖔 𝖑𝖚𝖗 𝖊𝖘𝖙 𝖔𝖗𝖙𝖆 𝖆𝖛𝖊 𝖗𝖊𝖌𝖎𝖓𝖆 𝖈𝖊𝖑𝖔𝖗𝖚𝖒 𝖊𝖙 𝖉𝖔𝖒𝖎𝖓𝖆 𝖆𝖓𝖌𝖊𝖑𝖔𝖗𝖚𝖒."

The tympanums on the outside are filled with chased ornaments and the sacred monogram. Under the bases of each leaf is a bracket-shaped finial of acanthus foliage ; in gilt metal. The whole diptych is a charming example of foliage and niello work, and the sculpture very good. The etching is about two-thirds the size of the original.

Bought for 25ol.

HORN, OR OLIPHANT.

IVORY.

No. 7953—1862.

IT is somewhat difficult to say to what country we should attribute this horn : it is Byzantine in general character, and was probably carved in some part of northern Europe by an artist of that school. The date is the eleventh century. What the original purpose may have been, whether for mere state or for actual use, is also uncertain.

This is a remarkably fine example of the kind. The outside is covered with interlacing circles, sharply cut, enclosing figures of various animals and birds in high relief. Many of these, as was usual in similar decorations of the tenth and eleventh centuries, are fabulous or grotesque ; but among them are an elephant, caparisoned, a stag, hares, and eagles. There are about thirty over the whole body of the horn. Each end is surrounded by a wide border, filled also with interlacing circles and animals.

The tusk has been hollowed throughout down to a slight thickness, scarcely more than sufficient to enable the artist to carve the design without piercing the ivory. In its present state, together with some light metal mountings at both extremities, the horn weighs six pounds and a quarter. It was formerly in the famous Soltikoff collection, dispersed in 1862. The length is two feet and an inch.

Several mediæval horns in ivory, among which a few may date as far back as the tenth century, are preserved in England ; generally they have been regarded and styled " tenure horns." Among these the most famous are the horn of Ulphus, in the treasury at York, and that given by Henry the First to the cathedral at Carlisle. Ivory horns, like caskets and rosaries and other ornaments, are frequent items in English inventories not only of churches and monasteries but of private families of the middle ages. There are two or three very fine examples in the Museum.

Bought for 193*l.*

CHRISMATORY.

SILVER, PARCEL GILT.

No. 7243—1861.

CHRISMATORIES of modern times are seldom made so rich or of so large a size (nearly eight inches) as the present example. They are among the most ancient of ecclesiastical vessels, and were in use among our Saxon forefathers in the 7th and 8th centuries. A chrismatory is intended to hold the three holy or sacred oils, which are hallowed by a bishop every year, on the Thursday in Holy week, and kept by all parish priests in communion with the Roman Church both in England and abroad, to be used as occasion requires. There are three kinds of oil thus blessed: one called chrism, to be put into the baptismal font and for other especial ceremonies, as (for instance) at confirmations, ordinations of priests, and coronations; the second, the oil for exorcisms, more especially, for the first unction at baptisms; the third, the oil for the sick, used only in giving the sacrament of extreme unction. The three oils are always most carefully kept, and in distinct flasks or small bottles.

This chrismatory is German work, probably late in the fifteenth century. The three small vases are cylindrical, and placed upright in the usual way. They are firmly bound together, above and below, with rims and lines of beaded and plain metal; the upper rim finished with a cresting of foliage, and the lower supported upon three lions. The cover, fitting closely into the upper rim, is divided by a long gilt acanthus leaf into three divisions, corresponding with each of the holy oils. The divisions have inscriptions incised on them; one "S. Cate:" for catechumens; another, "Chri," the chrism; and the third, "I," for the sick or infirm. The whole chrismatory is surmounted by a crucifix, of which the extremities of the cross are richly foliated; and the inscription INRI is not only put above the head of the Saviour, but is repeated on the back.

Between the cylindrical divisions are three crocketed and pinnacled canopies; under each is a small image. 1. The blessed Virgin and Child: 2. St. John the evangelist: 3. A saint vested as an archbishop. Inside is a flat plate, pierced with holes; intended to hold properly the separate small bottles, and marked for the chrism and the oils.

Bought for 70l.

I. 20

BOX IN CARVED OAK, FRENCH 18TH C.   14½ W × 8

BOX.

OAK.

No. 2528—1856.

THIS little casket is a good example of the best kind of architectural ornamentation, as applied in the fourteenth and fifteenth centuries to boxes, chests, and other furniture, whether of household or of ecclesiastical use. It may be either of French or of English work, about the year 1350.

The box is decorated throughout with geometric window tracery, filling the several panels, and with notchings on the angles. The clamps and mounts are iron, and of excellent workmanship. A hammered plate forms a clamp passing completely round the top edge under the cover, and finishing with a flower of beaten work on each side of the lock plate. The plate of the lock has foliated corners.

The size of the casket is nearly a foot long by about nine inches in width, and five inches high.

Bought for 2l.

PLAQUE.

BRASS.

No. 1217—1855.

THE centre of this charming piece of ornamental repoussé metal work, probably Flemish of the seventeenth century, represents a tulip in full flower surrounded by two rich floriated ornaments. The three are tied together with a band below. The etching is of the size of the original.

Excellent ornamental metal work in bronze and brass was produced in the Netherlands in the seventeenth and eighteenth centuries ; the style being for the most part modified by French taste, both in design and ornamentation.

Bought for 16s.

RELIEF IN THE DIFFUSION VELOREFERÉNER. H 19¼ W 6¾ IN
K N (*) 312¾ IN MIKE OFF *

LEAF OF A DIPTYCH.

IVORY.

No. 212—1865.

A NYTHING doubled or doubly folded is a diptych; and the term was commonly applied anciently to the tablets used for writing on with metallic or ivory styles. Sometimes these tablets had three leaves, sometimes five or more. In the first case they were then called triptychs, in the other pentaptychs or polyptychs. Examples of arrangements of both these last kinds are to be seen in the shrines of the middle ages.

When intended for writing-tablets the back of each leaf of the diptych was generally slightly hollowed in order to receive the wax for writing on. But not always; other modes (by a separate frame, for instance, attached to the leaves) were also used to preserve the wax from injury. We are therefore not to conclude that ivory diptychs so large as this were not intended for writing-tablets, or for the preservation of some family memoranda or records because the insides are smooth.

This leaf or plaque is Roman work of the third century, even if not of the second. Most of the large diptychs or portions of diptychs which have come down to our own times from that early period are what are called consular diptychs. These were made to form part of the presents commonly sent by the newly appointed consuls to eminent persons and to their own friends. About thirty of these consular diptychs, or leaves of them, are believed to exist now in various public and private collections. A perfect one of Probus Orestes and a leaf from a diptych of Anastasius are among the ivories in the Museum. Both are of a much later date; namely, of the sixth century. Another is in the Mayer collection at Liverpool; which also possesses two leaves claiming to be consular, but of which the genuineness is somewhat more than doubtful.

There is, probably, no carved antique ivory in the world which exceeds the leaf here engraved in interest or importance. And this, not only on account of its very early date, but from the beauty of its style and execution, and the fine state of its condition. Two narrow fractures of the border and of a small piece of a finger are the only injuries which it has suffered during the lapse of so many ages. The other leaf is preserved in the museum of the hôtel Cluny at Paris.

When kept together the two leaves had long been known and were famous. For centuries they formed the doors of a reliquary in the convent of Moutier in the diocese of Troyes, in France.   Gori described both in his Thesaurus, published about the year 1740.   They disappeared during the troubles of the French Revolution of 1790, and for many years were supposed to be lost.   Happily both have been discovered within the last thirty years.   The other leaf unfortunately is greatly injured ; having been found at the bottom of a well.   As a diptych the two leaves had names on labels at the top, on the one NICOMACHORVM, on the other SYMMACHORVM.   It is probable that it was originally made for a gift on the occasion of some marriage between members of the two patrician families ; or perhaps as a joint offering to the temple of Bacchus or of Cybele.

On this leaf a female, it may be a priestess, is represented standing before a low altar on which a fire is burning.   She is clothed from the shoulders to the feet in a long tunic, over which is thrown a pall or cloak, falling behind her over the left shoulder.   In one hand she holds a little open box from which she takes a grain, perhaps of incense, with the finger and thumb of the right hand, to drop it on the flame.   Her hair is bound with a fillet of ivy or small vine-leaves and gathered by a band into a knot behind the head.   On the wrist of either arm is a bracelet something like an East Indian bangle, and sandals on the feet.   The whole figure is extremely graceful and dignified ; the expression of the face earnest and devotional ; the form rightly expressed beneath the drapery, and the hands and feet well and carefully carved.

Behind the altar is a young female attendant, who holds a bowl in one hand and a two-handled cup in the other, both of which she presents to the priestess, looking up to her.   The girl is clothed in a single light garment. Behind, again, is an oak tree having several branches spreading over the head of the priestess, with very delicately executed leaves and acorns.

The altar is of the usual classic form, having on the top slab a wide scroll with volutes : the sides are ornamented with a bold wreath and fillets.   The whole subject is surrounded by a rich border of floriated ornaments interlacing.

The leaf preserved at Paris also represents a bacchante or priestess, but without an attendant : a pine tree, stiff in design and not to be compared with the oak on the South Kensington leaf, is behind the altar before which she stands.

The size of the leaf is eleven inches and three-quarters in length, and in width four inches and three-quarters.

Bought for 420*l.*

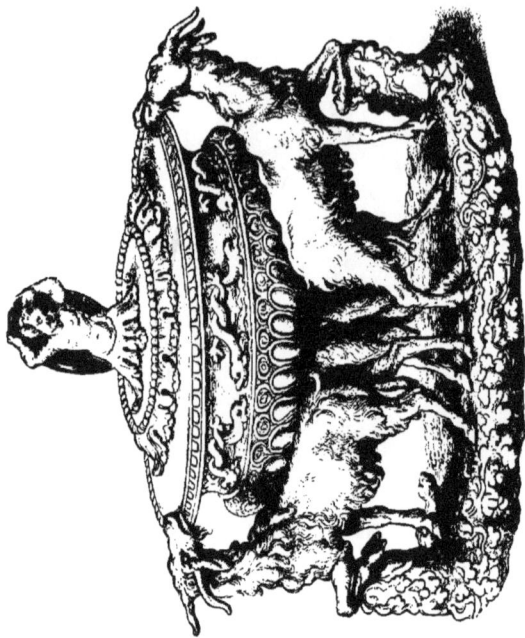

DESIGN FOR A SALT CELLAR.

From an original drawing attributed to Giulio Romano.

In the Art Library, South Kensington Museum.

DESIGN FOR A SALT-CELLAR.

No. 4900. Art Library.

A DRAWING in pen and bistre tint, ascribed to Giulio Romano. It is on paper, and was formerly in the famous collection of Dr. Wellesley, which was sold in 1866.

Three goats, each of which rests one leg on the trunk of a tree before him, support the salt-cellar. The base is decorated with leaves or scattered foliage, somewhat roughly indicated.

Giulio Romano (whose family name was Pippi) was born at Rome in 1492, and died in 1546. He was among the most distinguished of the pupils of Raffaelle.

·BETTER·IT·IS·TO·GET·WISDOM·THAN·GOLD·

DESIGN.

DOORWAY LEADING FROM QUADRANGLE.

A LL the decorations and figures of this doorway, which leads from the
centre quadrangle to the corridor near the refreshment rooms in the
Museum, were designed by the late Godfrey Sykes: the modellers were
J. Gamble and R. Townroe. The mouldings round the doorway are in
terra-cotta, executed by Blanchard and Co. Some small lizards crawling
over them, in relief, are worthy of especial notice.

The doors are of electrotyped bronze, gilt; by the late well-known
Giovanni Franchi. They contain in separate panels six figures, in high
relief, of men illustrious in Science and Art. Science occupies the left
side, and we have Davy, Newton, and Watt. The right hand panels show
Bramante, Michel Angelo, and Titian.

Over the doorway are typical figures of Science and Art, executed in
majolica by Minton and Hollins, which were also modelled by Gamble
and Townroe.

FRIEZE IN REFRESHMENT ROOM, SOUTH KENSINGTON MUSEUM, DESIGNED BY J. GAMBLE.

LAMP.

BRONZE.

No. 137.—1865.

THIS lamp, which was obtained at the sale of Lord Cadogan's collection in 1865, is in unusually good preservation. The decorations are numerous and varied ; designed with great spirit and executed by a good Florentine artist, in the early part (the best period) of the sixteenth century. Giovanni Rustici, a pupil of Verrocchio, Jacopo Sansovino, and others of the same school, produced many admirable works in bronze at that time ; but we cannot name the master to whom this lamp can be with certainty attributed.

The taste of the later part of the fourteenth and the beginning of the fifteenth centuries was greatly influenced by the admiration then spreading for the antique. The general idea of this lamp is borrowed from the shape of an ancient galley. The body is covered with reliefs : tritons and other fabulous marine animals, with a larger central subject in a medallion. Grotesque terminal figures, with foliated scrolls, fill the sweeps at the stern. Underneath, floral and other projections serve as supports. The rudder is equally rich in similar ornament ; and the cover is surmounted by a Cupid, riding upon a dolphin.

The height of the lamp is five inches, the length rather more than eight.

Bought for 163*l.*

I. 26

RELIQUARY.

ROCK CRYSTAL AND COPPER GILT.

No. 7946.—1862.

THIS admirable reliquary (formerly in the Soltikoff collection) is probably French, early in the fourteenth century. It stands about fourteen inches in height: twice the height and size represented in the
etching.

Originally, the reliquary seems to have been intended to hold four
relics, whether of different saints or of the same saint cannot now be deter-
mined. The two largest of these relics would be placed, one in the centre
at the top; the other in the half-circle (now glass, which has replaced
crystal) immediately above the base. Smaller relics were (almost certainly) preserved in the crystal turrets.

The reliquary is composed of two parts: a base or foot, with the
semicircular glass; above which is an architectural shrine, standing on
what some might call a sarcophagus, but which may rightly be described
as of the shape of a small portable altar. The base is square, with square
enamelled edges; these are divided into oblong compartments, two on each
side. One compartment has two small grotesque animals or monsters; the
other a leaf ornament with small stones set upon the face. Above this
the surface slopes inward up to a flat square, from which rises the stem
itself, two inches in height. This stem is enriched with a foliated
decoration.

The sloping surface of the concave below the stem has four compositions in low relief: they are not easily to be explained. On one side there
seems to be a representation of one of the legends connected with the life
of St. Jerome: and the saint is seen seated on an ass. A lion belonging
to the monastery was usually sent out to protect the ass in his service to
and fro: but having returned without his companion, which had been
stolen, was made by the monks to bear the ass's burthen. The lion is
here shown bringing back the ass; and one of the merchants who had
stolen it is entering through a door of the monastery. In another com-

I. 27

partment a king is seated between two abbots at the entrance of an abbey, of which the doors are sculptured with images, pinnacles, &c. Another abbot, or bishop, draws a man out of the mouth of a well. On the third side a bishop is giving the tonsure to a youth whose mother presents him. Two bishops are placing a mitre on the head of an ecclesiastic vested in an alb. The fourth side is shown in the etching. A man, kneeling, offers a reliquary to a king sitting on his throne. Two women, standing behind, also carry reliquaries or little shrines, waiting their turn to offer. Behind these, again, are three servants bringing in chests containing other offerings.

The semicircular piece of glass on which the small altar rests still contains what appears to be a fragment of a skull. The upper part of the little altar or sarcophagus slides ; and beneath it is a rectangular space, in which there is at present a small relic, which seems from the date of an inscription on it to be of much later time than the reliquary ; probably deposited by a pious possessor in the last century. The sides are filled with eight double windows under arches, having a projecting cornice above and below. The surfaces are covered with metal work beaten into small flowers, with pieces of silver niello ornament at intervals. Above the altar is a square, richly decorated panel finishing above with a gable, and supported on each side with a round turret or buttress, the shafts being crystal. In the centre of the panel is a circular case covered with a crystal, in which probably the chief relic was originally deposited. On the back is an incised figure of the Virgin and Child, with a background of floriated ornament in niello. The enrichments of the whole panel consist of filigree silver work, enclosing a number of crystals and precious stones. The turrets at the angles are topped by conical roofs of metal work.

Bought for 130*l.*

CABINET.

WALNUT-WOOD.

No. 772—1865.

OF French art, this cabinet dates from about the year 1550. At that period the renaissance in France had advanced far beyond the extent to which it had been received in England and Flanders. Francis the First had not only sent workmen to be educated in Florence and Rome, but had invited artists out of Italy to teach in different schools as architects, painters, and sculptors. The names of Primaticcio and Cellini occur to us at once, and prove how great must have been the influence which they exercised.

The present example of French woodwork of that period is one of the best in the large and important collection gathered together in the Museum. It is extremely well composed in outline, with justly proportioned and arranged mouldings, and with decorations admirably suited to the object.

The cabinet is made up in two stages, the upper receding nearly eight inches from the top of the lower. It has side offsets, which supply a richer character than mere upright mouldings; and the diminution of width and depth, giving a lightness to what is, in fact, a large piece of furniture, is worth careful observation. The lower portion forms a cupboard, with a pair of drawers over it. It is lifted from the ground by broad horizontal mouldings which, being the widest measure of the whole piece, serve in the way of gradation to the other parts as they rise up. Four stout feet with claws support the two front corners.

The doors of the cupboard are panelled, with projecting outside mouldings, cut into small egg and tongue on the inside. The flat parts of the panels are covered with a tracery in marquetry of delicate foliage and flowers, springing from vases. The side framing-piece and the drawer-fronts are inlaid in like manner; and the top is carried on a mask in the centre with brackets at the corners.

The top half of the cabinet contains two drawers and two cupboards, as below. But the drawers are, in this case, placed below the cupboards, and

I. 28

these last are, of necessity, much narrower. A wide side margin of three inches surrounds the cupboard doors, and above them spreads a projecting moulded cornice. The cornice is supported at the corners by four grotesque human-headed terminal figures. Their bodies bulge outwards in the centre and recede again, so as to fall in, bracket-shaped, down to a horizontal parcel of string-mouldings which keeps the whole together. Beneath this string the terminal supports descend in claw feet spreading upon the table of the lower cupboards.

The top piece under the cornice is fronted with arabesques and small figures in relief connecting baskets of flowers at each corner, and a tablet with marble inlay forms the centre. Above the cornice (but not shown in the etching) is a pierced pedimental composition of two human-headed winged dragons, with arabesques, strapwork, &c., above which is a pelican feeding her young. This stands out on the front edge of the cabinet.

It is impossible to say by what artist this cabinet was designed. Jean Goujon, whose sculptures still remain on the Louvre, stands at the head of the French masters of that time. Others were Philibert de L'Orme and Bachelier of Toulouse. To the last of these the present example has been, with great probability, attributed.

The cabinet is seven feet ten inches high, by three feet eight inches long, and one foot ten inches wide. It was formerly in the Soulages collection.

Bought for 200*l.*

.

HEAD OF A PASTORAL STAFF.

IVORY.

No. 214.—1865.

THIS is a very splendid example of a class of carvings in ivory which is extremely rare ; nor is it easy to say why this should be the case. In the middle ages there must have been many crosier-heads made in ivory as well as in metal or in silver. The cost would have had no effect in diminishing the number : for ivory, in pieces of the size required, would have been little less costly than silver, and considerably more than metal. Even if the general destruction in England of all ecclesiastical ornaments in the sixteenth century would account for the rarity now of these things in our own country, yet we can scarcely give the same reason for the smallness of the number still known to exist abroad. We find comparatively very few in the great collections at Paris, or Vienna, or elsewhere.

The difficulty is increased when we remember that not only bishops but the heads of religious houses, both in England and abroad, carried these staffs as emblems of their authority ; and scarcely anything is found more frequently than an entry of an ivory crosier or staff in mediæval inventories.

Ivory, as a material, is admirably adapted for the crooks of pastoral staffs ; and not only so, but admits of very graceful work in the decoration and applying of the appropriate symbols. Very anciently, the shape was simple, in the plain form of a shepherd's crook ; then treated as a serpent of which the termination was the head, often with widely expanded jaws ; later on, many symbolic ornaments were added, and groups of figures were carved in relief, not only upon the volute, but introduced into and filling up the centre.

This crosier-head is French, of the best period of the fourteenth century. In height, six inches and three-quarters ; in width, nearly four ; somewhat larger than it is represented in the etching. The whole of it is carved from a single piece of ivory.

The outside of the volute is ornamented with a very richly designed branch of a vine, cut in high relief, and of admirable workmanship : there

I. 29

are, here and there, a few small bunches of fruit. The volute is supported by an angel, designed with great spirit, whose wings on one side spread to the inner angle, and his hands stretch forward towards a scroll in front. He is vested in a long garment, under which are seen the feet, on the side not shown in the etching.

The centre is entirely filled with two groups, standing (as it were) back to back. On one side is the Crucifixion. Our Lord is represented dead, with His head drooping over the body ; on His right hand is the blessed Virgin, on the other is St. John. Both these are standing. On the reverse are the Virgin and Child with two angels, grouped in the manner common in the fourteenth century. The Virgin holds the Infant on her left arm, and the angels attend, one on each side, carrying candlesticks. They are all fully draped in long vestments.

The mediæval ivory heads of episcopal staffs show often great cleverness in adapting two groups for the centre, so that one of the two might face the people as it was carried along. In the present example, the figures which serve upon the one side for the Crucifixion, represent upon the other the blessed Virgin and the attendant angels.

Bought for 168l.

M A C E.

S I L V E R.

No. 31—1869.

E NGLISH work, late in the seventeenth century. The stem is twisted with two knops—one, the largest, in the middle ; the other at the bottom, near the end. The foot is a flattened cone, bearing underneath the arms of the city of Cork : a ship entering a port between two towers, in full sail.

The middle knop, which is quite round, has four figures : Temperance, Fortitude, Justice, and Prudence. These are in relief, within circles.

The head is a regal crown, surmounted by a cross and supported by an octagonal bracket, which grows out of the stem. Upon this bracket are eight shields. These may possibly have been those of other corporations or companies connected with that to which the mace belonged. For example, among them is a shield bearing a covered cup between two candlesticks, with a device, two hands issuing from a cloud and holding pincers. Another has, on a chevron, between three tents, three cinquefoils ; for a device, a tent-head, and for supporters, two boys. Another, on a chevron, three cinquefoils between three grates ; for a device, two arms upraised, holding a dish, and a motto, " In God is all my trust." To name one more only : this bears a tobacco-plant in full blossom, proper ; for a device, a demi-man, with arms extended, holding a pipe and a cake of tobacco ; for supporters, two savage men, cinctured with leaves.

On the crown is a hall-mark, R. C., a castle and flagstaff, and a galleon. There is also the following legend : " *This mace was made at y^e charge of y^e whole Sosiety of Gouldsmiths, Robert Goble, M^{tr}. W^{tr}. Hughet, W^{tr}. Harvy, Ward^{ns},* 1696."

The length is an inch and a-half over three feet, the width of the crown about five inches.

Bought for 73l. 10s.

CASKET.

COPPER: ENAMELLED.

No. 4.—1865.

THERE are very few objects in the collections of the Museum which are more important or of higher historical interest than this casket. It is English work of the end of the thirteenth century, and was probably made for Valence Earl of Pembroke.

The enamelling is like that of Limoges, which came largely into use about the year 1200 and was applied constantly in the way of decoration to all kinds of metal work of moderate size. Reliquaries, pastoral staffs, candlesticks, basins, jewels, and coffers, were richly ornamented with enamel : occasionally, also, monumental brasses.

This casket is flat, and stands on four legs rudely and plainly shaped. It is entirely of copper-gilt and covered with champlevé enamel ; displaying the armorial shields, in lozenge or diamond-shaped compartments, of England, Angoulême, Dreux Duke of Brittany, and Valence Earl of Pembroke. These compartments touch at the points, with small quatrefoil ornaments at the points of intersection. The shields have the following heraldic bearings repeated throughout :—

1. Sable, a lion rampant, or. 2. Barry of twelve, argent and azure, six martlets, gules, for Aymer de Valence. 3. Checquy, argent and sable, the second charged with crosses patée, or, in dexter chief a canton ermine. 4. Checquy diamondwise, or and gules. 5. Or, a lion rampant, gules. All the colours are in fair preservation, some even bright, and easily to be distinguished.

Besides the shields there is no decoration, except a narrow Vandyke-fashioned border round the edges of each side. The hinges are round bars, shaped at the ends, as was very common at that period, into dragons' heads ; they are welded on over the lid and back. The lock is a similar bar with a hasp hinged to it ; having an inside lock, locked through a key-hole. A well-designed and properly-sized handle serves to raise the lid.

The casket is about seven inches long, by five and a quarter wide. It stands nearly four inches high.

Bought for 150*l.*

MARBLE PANEL (N° 514-73)
ITALIAN FIFTEENTH CENTURY

PANEL.

MARBLE.

No. 314—1878.

T HIS panel is almost square in shape, and the subject is carved in low
relief. It is of the school of Donatello, Italian, of the early part of
the fifteenth century. It was obtained from the Lazzari palace at Padua.

In the centre, the Blessed Virgin is seated, holding the dead body of
our Lord on her lap, and supporting His head with her left hand, whilst
her right arm, passed across her breast, lifts Him up beneath His shoulder.
This portion of the composition is in the common style of a Pietà of the
middle ages.

But the group which is gathered round the two chief figures is treated
in a very unusual manner : nor is it easy to suggest whom the figures are
intended to represent. Five, in the background, stand upright and are
men ; probably two or three of them (more especially the second man on
the left hand, whose face is seen in profile) are portraits. A portion of the
foot of the Cross would seem to be indicated, as if embraced by the man
standing in the middle of the group of five. If this be so, the whole
subject would be the Deposition : an interpretation in full accordance with
the gestures and arrangement of the lower group of figures, which consists
of four women. Two of these stand behind the Blessed Virgin with
clasped hands, in an attitude of great grief ; a third, kneeling, almost
touches with her lips, in a posture of adoration, the Saviour's knees ; a
fourth, an old woman sitting on the ground, tenderly lifts up the left
hand of the dead body, wrapped reverentially in a portion of her robe. Three
of the women, and the Blessed Virgin also, have their heads covered with
the draperies of their outer robes, in the manner of a hood under which is
a kind of low veil, almost hiding the eyes and passing straight across
the forehead. The kneeling figure on the left alone has her head un-
covered, and possibly is meant for St. Mary Magdalen.

This marble is a very fine and very rare example of the school to
which it belongs, and deserves to be most carefully studied.

The group of women who weep round the dead Saviour is full of
character and feeling, and the execution admirable throughout. The

I. 32

draperies, the feet and hands of the figures, the varied expression of the faces, and the solemn grandeur of the head and body of our Lord, will bear comparison with the best works of a somewhat later time.

The panel measures three feet four inches in height, by about three feet seven in width.

Bought for 300l.

VIEW

ACROSS THE CENTRAL OR LOAN COURT.

CAPTAIN FOWKE, R.E. (who died in December, 1865) designed this court, which was opened in 1862; and the decorations are by Godfrey Sykes. Brown relieved with gold and blue with white form the key of the scale of colour. All the iron columns, ribs, and girders are exposed to view and have been treated as surfaces for decoration; even the bolts and rivets form ornamental details.

On the upper part are shown some of the portraits, in mosaic, of men connected with the arts from the earliest times to the present.

PANEL OF WINDOW FRAME,
SOUTH KENSINGTON MUSEUM.
Designed by Godfrey Sykes.

I. 33

KNOCKER.

BRONZE.

No. 588—1853.

THIS is one of a pair of knockers which were formerly on the large doors of the palazzo Martinengo-dobblo at Brescia; and the companion knocker was still hanging there within the last few years. It is probably Venetian work, of about the middle of the sixteenth century.

Venice seems to have relied until the fifteenth century for whatever bronze work she might require upon the supply which she was able to procure through her intercourse with Constantinople. Even in instances which may be found where the artists employed worked at home, very strong Byzantine feeling and marked style are to be traced ; as, for example, in one of the doors of St. Mark's, made as early as the twelfth century. But later on, the influence of the schools of Squarcione and Mantegna made itself felt ; and still more powerfully the inspiration which spread all over the north of Italy from the studio of Donatello. By the beginning of the sixteenth century Venetian workers in bronze had established a wide renown ; and to Alessandro Leopardi may be attributed, with almost certainty, considerable portions of the famous equestrian statue of Bartolomeo Colleoni. Later still, Jacopo Sansovino, Alessandro della Volpe, and Titiano Aspetti worked at Venice. To either of these or to their pupils this knocker may be ascribed, even if it be thought somewhat too late in style to be given to Leopardi himself. Although small works in bronze, like inkstands, knockers, or ornamental furniture, carry with them certain characteristics of style, approximately indicating the hand which modelled them, yet very often it is impossible to set them down with absolute certainty to any particular artist.

In this splendid knocker the composition is formed by two dolphins, which extend, one on each side, from a winged mask of Medusa at the top.

I. 34

Each dolphin is entwined with a serpent and supports a satyr, whose truncated arms, ending in curled scrolls, are hooked into a blank escutcheon which forms the centre of the group. A small tragic mask, uniting the heads of the dolphins, completes the lower portion.

This example is one of the most artistic and vigorous of those which still exist. Large and heavy as they are, nevertheless, when fixed to the huge doors of the great Italian palaces, they harmonize perfectly with the proportions and architecture of the buildings for which they were designed. The height is fourteen inches by eleven in width.

Bought for 21l.

BELLOWS.

WOOD.

No. 7698—1861.

ITALIAN artists in the sixteenth century did not confine themselves to the designing and executing important works, but were also ready to give their aid to the making of furniture, chests, cabinets, tables, &c., in every variety of material and with all kinds of decoration. Even things which one would suppose to be intended only for the commonest domestic use were not beneath their notice. Wood was very frequently employed : and it was ornamented with rich carvings, or with gilding and painting ; inlaid with agate, lapis lazuli, or other precious marbles; or with ivory, tortoise-shell, and mother-of-pearl.

The bellows here engraved is Italian of about the middle of the sixteenth century : formerly in the Soulages collection, and an admirable example of excellent design and bold carving in high relief applied to a common object.

The front forms a circular cartouche with scroll ends curled over, half covering a border richly made up with fruit and flowers. The panel has at the top a mask, and the centre is filled with two dolphins, their tails continuing in scrolls which roll over and terminate in demi-figures of men with shields and wielding clubs. The arms on one shield are, bendy of six with a lion rampant over all : on the other a double-headed imperial eagle displayed, bearing an inescutcheon charged with a fesse. Where the bodies of the dolphins leave a space in their sweep towards each other is a scallop-shell, answering to the mask above. A squatting female figure, winged, is carved upon the handle. The body of the bellows rests upon an eagle standing, with outstretched wings: well executed and vigorous in design.

The back of the bellows has also a cartouche, with masks, shells, &c., supporting it. The wind-pipe is formed by a grotesque animal (issuing from a satyr's head) with wings and with the fore paws under its throat. The old undressed buff-leather is still left on the edges, fastened to the wood with rosette-shaped nails of bronze.

The diameter of the bellows is rather less than eleven inches.

Bought for 40l.

MONSTRANCE.

GILT METAL.

No. 4310—1857.

A N important piece of Spanish work, about the beginning of the
sixteenth century. Important, not only on account of having a date
and of the very characteristic style of the design, but because also of the
material of which it is made. Spanish mediæval work in bronze or copper
is more rare than in silver or iron. Bronze lamps, mortars, and perfume-
burners, and some representations of animals, are preserved in a few
museums, but these are almost all to be referred to Spanish-Moresque
artists and workmen. The famous and beautiful "tenebrarium," or
triangular candlestick (used during matins in Holy-week for the fifteen
tapers) kept in the cathedral at Seville is the most remarkable work in
bronze ever executed in Spain. This was made in 1562 by Bartolomé
Morel, an artist who was contemporary with the maker of the monstrance
shown in the etching.

The monstrance is designed as an architectural shrine of three or four
stories. The plan of the body is triangular, and the shrine is built upon a
platform curving inwards. Three terminal figures of prophets, wearing
turbans and holding scrolls, stand on square dado bases covered with
arabesques in relief. Upon the scrolls is an inscription : "*Adorate
scabellum pedum ejus quoniam sanctus est.*" Behind these figures are
columns with Corinthian capitals to which are attached little angels, who
seem to be flying downwards and holding censers with which they
incense the Host. The columns and figures together support architraves
and cornices richly decorated and divided into panels, which run con-
tinuously round the entire piece.

Above this another little temple or shrine is raised. This is round,
marked as if with courses of stone, and divided by three piers which
are faced by columns, supported on the outside by well-designed, bold,

scroll-shaped brackets. Three round-headed arches contain three images: 1. The Redeemer holding an orb in one hand and raising the other in benediction. 2. The blessed Virgin with the Infant in her arms. 3. St. John the Baptist. Upon the same floor, outside the brackets, are three small figures of bishops, vested and mitred and holding pastoral staffs. They hold also, one a book, another a rosary, and the third a heart pierced with two nails.

Again, resting upon this round shrine is placed a drum covered by a smaller dome standing on six balusters, and the summit carries a crucifix. This crucifix is double, having a figure on both sides of the cross. The actual receptacle for the Host is an upright cylinder of glass, occupying the centre of the lowest story; and the metal support is a double image, the Virgin and Child with a kneeling bishop, and the Assumption.

The stem is straight, with a large knob or boss in the middle by which to raise the monstrance safely; the whole of it enriched with medallions in strap-work. Below this the foot spreads, having not only the same kind of ornament, but also three circular medallions, and three settings for gems or coloured pastes. In the medallions are the evangelists, St. Matthew, St. Luke, and St. John.

The height of the monstrance is twenty-one inches.

Bought for 60*l.*

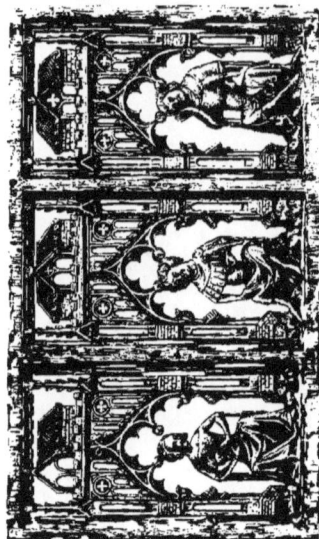

PANELS.

IVORY.

No. 284—1867.

N OT only because of the good workmanship and graceful design shown in them, or because there are few pieces more characteristic of the period and style when they were carved, but because they are examples of English art, these small panels are extremely valuable and important. Originally, it is probable that they formed the decoration of a very beautiful small casket, of which the three panels in one piece made the front or back. The date is about the middle of the fourteenth century.

The panel is divided into three compartments; in each of them is a sitting figure. In one is a lady caressing a dog; in the others two gentlemen, both carrying a hawk upon the wrist. All three have the long narrow strips hanging from their sleeves; and the men show also the pointed shoe of the time of Edward the Third, which was worn before the fashion came in of the exaggerated elongation beyond the foot.

Each figure is placed under a rich canopy; an ogee arch with bold cusps floriated at the points and supported by pinnacled turrets or buttresses at the sides. Carried upon the arches is a battlemented wall with windows, and above this a low-roofed building with a gable in the middle. The whole of the architectural decoration is delicately cut in open or pierced work.

The fragment to the left is a portion of one of the sides, with the sitting figure of a lady.

The piece with the three panels is five inches long, and five wide.

Bought for 10*l.*

BOOK CLASPS, &c.   FELT,   16TH CEN. GER. (No. 118)
BOOK CLASPS, A   CHASED SILVER, HEART-SHAPED ENDS

BOOK-CLASPS.

SILVER.

Nos. 3583—1853, and 9019—1863.

THE centre clasp is intended for a single one to close a book, and is a good example of French design and workmanship of about the year 1690. The material is silver, which has been gilded; the decoration is with filigree work, surrounding three small plaques of champlevé enamel in niello. The clasp is rather over five inches in length from point to point, but the same design could easily be adapted for books either of larger or smaller size.

The other two clasps are a pair, to be fitted across the edges near the top and bottom of the binding. They are also silver, very carefully chased with scroll or foliated ornaments and heart-shaped ends. It is not easy to determine where they were made, but at some time early in the last century. The etching represents the size of the originals.

Bought for 3l. 11s. 8d.

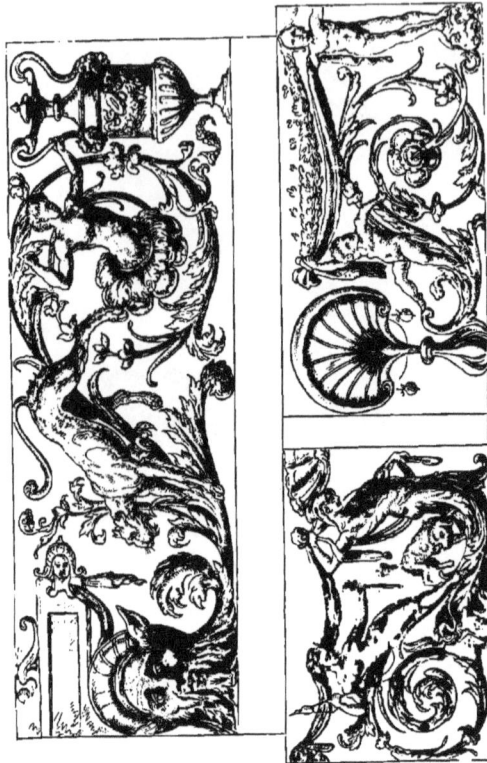

THREE DESIGNS FOR PANELS BY GIOVANNI DA UDINE PLATE
IN THE ART LIBRARY SOUTH KENSINGTON MUSEUM

THREE DESIGNS FOR PANELS.

No. 8076. Art Library.

THESE are pen and bistre drawings, perhaps designs for friezes, and are ascribed to Giovanni da Udine. They are upon paper, by the same hand but not on the same sheet.

Giovanni Nanni, called "da Udine," was born at Udine in 1494; and at an early age was placed under the tuition of Giorgione at Venice. From thence he went to Rome, where he was employed by Raffaelle to execute the greater part of the arabesque and grotesque ornaments in stucco by which the apartments in the Vatican are decorated. He died at Rome in 1564.

EAGLE.

IRON.

No. 603—1875.

A MAGNIFICENT example of Japanese work in iron. The bird, an eagle or osprey, stands with spread feet and out-stretched wings upon a rock, eagerly looking, as if preparing to swoop downwards on his prey. The body and wings are composed of numberless pieces of iron, some cast and others cut and hammered, with chasing.

The name of the artist is known—Miyôchin Munéharu. He lived in the sixteenth century, and his works are especially valued in Japan. The height is two feet four inches and a half, and the expanse of the wings three feet one inch.

Bought for 1,000*l.*

1.47

DESIGN:

DECORATIONS OF THE WEST DINING-ROOM.

M ORRIS AND CO. designed and executed these decorations. The engraving shows portions of the upper panels of the dado. The figures represent the twelve months of the year or the signs of the zodiac with two additional personifications of the sun and the moon. The intermediate panels are filled with fruit and foliage.

The two figures engraved show Libra or September, and the Moon.

PANEL IN WINDOW RECESS, SOUTH KENSINGTON MUSEUM.

Designed by Godfrey Sykes.

BOOK COVER. METAL GILT. S CENT.
FRAGMENT OF A BOOK.
W. LAWSON fecit.

BOOK COVER.

GILT-METAL UPON WOOD.

No. 1057—1871.

EXAMPLES of undoubtedly English work in metal of this date, early in the fourteenth century, are rare, and the book-cover shown in the etching is an extremely important specimen. Even if we had no guide to lead us in the manuscript which it contains, there is a peculiar and characteristic style, both in the workmanship and in the design, which would leave us in very little doubt as to the country in which it was made.

The manuscript is English of about the year 1400; including the office for the dead (the dirge and placebo), also the office for anniversaries, and a portion (the sequences) of the mass for All Souls' day.

The centre panel, which is somewhat recessed, represents the Visitation; the Virgin and St. Elizabeth stand facing each other vested in ample robes, and with hands clasped in each other's in the front. These figures are in high relief. Behind them is shown a gateway of a town, with flanking towers.

Eight plates of metal work fixed to the wood with pins form a border round the central compositions. They are decorated with a rich and well-designed flamboyant tracery within panels, in pierced or open work. Four antique gems are set in the corners, surrounded by a somewhat bolder ornament of foliage. One of these gems has a hand upon it in relief, two are cut in intaglio, and one is plain.

The cover measures about ten inches, by seven in width.

Bought for 3d.

I. 42

FIRE-DOG.

BRONZE.

No. 3011—1857.

ONE of a pair of fire-dogs : the difference between the two being that the figure upon this represents Jupiter, on the other Venus. The height is three feet and a half.

The modelling is bold and the ornamentation rich, almost overdone ; but the base is not sufficiently solid. The composition is arranged in four stages ; the decorations consisting of festoons, masks, and terminal figures.

These fire-dogs are important from their size and from the signature of the maker, inscribed on the back : " Josepho di Levi in Verona mi fece."

Their date is the sixteenth century.

Bought for 151*l. the pair.*

i

J. 43

BOX OR SMALL COFFER.

WOOD AND IVORY.

No. 532—1869.

A RATHER remarkable specimen of the peculiar work not uncommon in the north of Italy from about the middle of the fifteenth to the middle of the sixteenth century. This casket is probably Venetian about the year 1500, and is made of olive-wood. The top is arched or cylindrical, and the whole is decorated with reticulations pierced right through, alternately long and short but not over half an inch in the longest of these dimensions. This pattern work without exactly following the cuspings of English fifteenth century tracery has much the same general effect. The panels are divided by crossing bands of ivory, engraved with lines in simple knots.

The box measures five inches by six inches and a half.

Bought for 12*l.*

CUP.

SILVER.

No. 150—1872.

A CUP of Nuremberg work which has been attributed by some whose authority deserves consideration to Jamnitzer, a goldsmith admitted into the Nuremberg guild about 1534. The etching is about three-fourths the height of the original.

The bowl of the cup stands on a baluster-shaped stem, and is cusped at the lip in six lobes descending in points; the intervals as they increase in width are filled with good taste by six corresponding lobes, ascending till the points are lost between the cuspings of the lip. Small subjects in repoussé work are embossed below the points under the cup. They represent three fishes, a lizard, a frog, a prawn, a dolphin, and a snail. The surfaces of the lobes which diminish upwards are covered with strapwork and cartouches containing three demi-figures alternating with arabesque ornaments. The upper and larger lobes have graceful figures of Diana with a bow, Lucretia with a dagger, and a third of doubtful meaning, said (but improbably) to be Judith with the head of Holofernes. Three vases intervene. The edge of the lip for about an inch is quite plain: and immediately under the cusps masks and arabesque work are placed alternately.

The base of the cup is trefoil-shaped with a bold half torus. The knop in the middle resembles the capital of a renaissance column, with three rams' heads, three bunches of fruit, and volutes. This stands on a round basket connected with the base by three dolphin-shaped brackets. The stem, which is hexagonal and divided by horizontal collars and neckings, is connected with the bowl by six delicate acanthus brackets.

The condition of this cup is as good as when it came from the hand of the maker, and it must have been very little used. Two cups of similar workmanship belong to the municipal collection at Nuremberg, and are shown in the town-hall. The three (this and the other two) were exhibited together at Nuremberg at the 400th anniversary of Albert Dürer, in 1871.

Wentzel Jamnitz or Jamnitzer was the author of a work on perspective with cuts by Jost Amman, and was one of a family of gold and silver-smiths. There is some correspondence of style and execution between the three cups and a very beautiful cup preserved in the British Museum, and believed to be by Cellini; but which, with more probability, is the work either of Wentzel or an artist of the same school.

I. 45   *Bought for* 150*l.*

IVORY CARVING, HEAD OF A TAU OR T SHAPED STAFF, IN WALRUS
TUSK, THE COMPARTMENTS CONTAINING THE SIGNS OF THE
ZODIAC. 12ᵗʰ CENT (SOLTIKOFF COLL) I, 5 IN. S.K.M. (Nº 215 '65)
F.A.SLOCOMBE FECIT

HEAD OF A TAU.

IVORY.

No. 215 —1865.

THE Tau was one form of the heads of pastoral staffs adopted in some countries of western Europe early in the middle ages : the use of it seems to have died out soon after the eleventh century ; but it can be traced back almost to primitive times. The most ancient shape of the episcopal staff is to be found represented in the catacombs ; a short handle with a plain end slightly curved. Soon after, and this also in the catacombs, the truer form of a shepherd's crook occurs, with a complete and still unornamented curve at the extremity of the staff. Succeeding all these simpler forms came the admirable design, frequently executed in the thirteenth and fourteenth centuries, in which the volute is carried half round again and filled within the circle with religious emblems or with groups of figures.

Ivory taus are of great rarity ; and no other collection, whether public or private, can boast of a finer or more important example. It is carved out of walrus ivory : in some country of western or northern Europe, and possibly may be English art late in the eleventh century. The two ends are lost ; probably they represented the heads of animals, and may have been hollowed out in order to hold relics.

The sides are divided into diamond-shaped compartments, in each of which is carved, in high relief, a sign of the zodiac. The bands which separate these compartments are richly ornamented with small beads ; and a larger circle or hollow at the intersections was originally, without much doubt, filled with gems. Smaller animals (some of them hares or birds, some grotesque beasts) occupy the smaller divisions where portions only of the diamond compartments can find room.

In the centre of the under part is a round opening, into which the up-

I. 46

right staff was fitted : on either side is a niche under canopies of three small round arches supported on columns with early Norman capitals.

In one there stands (it seems) an abbot tonsured, vested in an alb and short chasuble, holding a book in his left hand, and in the right a short pastoral staff with the crook turned towards himself. Under the other canopy stands another ecclesiastic vested in like manner, who carries a tau in his left hand ; a long staff with a short cross-piece at the top. With the right hand he gives benediction. He is also tonsured. There is an ornament upon the front of his chasuble which might be supposed to represent an archbishop's pall ; but more probably it is an orphrey of the vestment.

The length of the tau is five inches, and the width nearly two.

Bought for 77l.

KNIFE CASE.

WOOD, PAINTED.

No. 2156—1855.

A N Italian work, and important as having a date, 1564. The case is formed by three satyrs bound with linen bands to a triangular pedestal which rests upon three harpies. The satyrs are black, with horse's hoofs, and two of them are dressed with Indian feather skirts. The triangular pedestal is painted the colour of Siena marble. The sphinx on the top holds a scutcheon by the left paw ; but the arms once painted on it cannot now be blazoned. The head turns slightly and is crowned with bay leaves. There are some imitation jewels on the base, painted in glazes over gilding.

The case was bought from the Bernal collection in 1855, and stands about fourteen inches high. The date is on a small scutcheon in the centre of the base.

Bought for 10*l.* 10*s.*

PAPE NICOLA X
ASER NAD TO BERNINI
LA CAN GALLERI

h-48

BUST.

BRONZE.

No. 1088—1853.

A PORTRAIT bust in bronze, considerably larger than life, of pope Innocent the tenth, Gian. Battista Pamfili, of Rome; who was elected in 1644 and died in 1655. It is Italian and contemporary. The artist is unknown; more probably he was Alessandro Algardi, who died in 1654, than Bernini to whom the work has been by some ascribed.

The pope wears a plain close-fitting cap upon his head, and a vestment which may, possibly, be intended for a cope; the border of the vestment is decorated with olive-branches intertwined so as to form circles, containing alternately a fleur-de-lis and a dove, the emblems of the family.

The workmanship and modelling are both good; and the finishing of the casting and tooling also excellent. Probably the bust was executed when pope Innocent was a cardinal, as there is no emblem upon it having reference to the papal chair and dignity.

The height is three feet three inches, by two feet ten inches in width.

Bought for 90l.

I. 48

THE CERAMIC GALLERY, SOUTH KENSINGTON MUSEUM

INTERIOR OF THE CERAMIC GALLERY.

I N this gallery (which was opened in 1868) are exhibited the museum collections of various kinds of pottery and porcelain, chiefly European.
The decorations are partly from designs by the late Godfrey Sykes, but
chiefly by others, among whom Mr. J. Gamble and Mr. F. W. Moody may
especially be named. They are intended to illustrate in some degree the
special purpose for which the gallery was built. For example, the columns
which support the roof are of enamelled terra cotta, executed by Minton
& Co. ; they are white and celadon green with capitals partly gilt. Round
each pillar is a band bearing the name of some celebrated potter. On the
frieze are the names of places where pottery has been, or is now, manufac-
tured; and the windows on the north side, designed by Mr. W. B. Scott,
contain a series of pictures giving the history of the manufacture of china
and pottery in different ages and countries.

The large object in the foreground of the etching is a green earthenware stove from the Black Forest.

PANEL, FROM A DESIGN BY GODFREY SYKES.

GLORIA IN EXCELSIS DEO
ET IN TERRA PAX

I. 60

PAX.

SILVER GILT.

No. 3580—1856.

THE design and composition of this pax are of the character of similar objects by Italian artists, to which school about 1550 the design belongs. The centre panel represents the Nativity, with the blessed Virgin and St. Joseph kneeling on either side of the infant Saviour. Two half-angels behind the manger join in an attitude of adoration, and two shepherds are seen at the back of the Virgin. This is executed in niello. The frame stands upon a dado and is supported by flanking brackets. Two side pilasters filled with arabesque work of great delicacy support the entablature. The tympanum contains a representation, also in niello, of the Eternal Father with arms extended and surrounded by angels. The dado is filled with a light arabesque ornament; and on the entablature is the legend " *Gloria in excelsis Deo, et in terra pax.*" The size is eight inches in height by about five across.

The pax is used at high mass in the catholic Church : very frequent notices of it are to be found in mediæval inventories, and in service books of the Church of England before the reign of Edward the sixth. Several examples in metal and in ivory are preserved in the museum.

Bought for 100*l.*

GERMAN 17 CENT 1441 N . SK N N 31 N

CASKET.

SILVER.

No. 2126—1855.

THE workmanship of this pretty casket is probably north Italian rather than German, and the date about the end of the sixteenth century. The shape and style might very usefully be adapted to various common things of the same kind at the present day.

The whole surface is covered with filigree; each depression being filled with enamel of different colours—turquoise blue, yellow dots, and deep purple. The feet are well designed, and give a good character to the casket; they represent grotesque figures, something like a sphinx.

The height is four and a half inches, by nearly six long, and three and a half wide.

Bought for 38*l.*

152.

MIRROR FRAME.

WALNUT WOOD.

No. 7226—1860.

THIS fine specimen of wood-work, Italian of the sixteenth century, is
useful not only as a type and style which may be copied or adapted
for the same purpose, namely, for a mirror frame, but also for other articles
of furniture ; for panels of cabinets and the like. Mirrors in our own
time are very much larger in proportion to the frames.

The plate is metal, burnished, and is partly covered by a sunk sliding
panel admirably carved in slight relief with a profile female head in classic
costume. The frame is richly carved also in relief with masks and garlands
of fruits and flowers resting on a bracket and surmounted by a cornice.
On each side is the head of a boy, with a scroll of acanthus leaves above
and below. The flat portions of the frame are inlaid with what appears
to be cork, but is perhaps cut from the excrescences of a chestnut tree.
Originally the large bracket had armorial bearings carved upon the shield
which occupies the centre ; but these have been defaced. This frame
formed part of the Soulages collection.

The height is nearly three feet and a half, by two feet two inches in
width.

Bought for 20*l.*

l. 52

VASE.

B R O N Z E.

No. 35—1865.

A VERY beautiful work of the Italian school of the latter half of the sixteenth century. The body of the vase is cylindrical, diminishing towards the foot with a bold gadroon ornament. The cylinder itself has a rich foliated decoration of an antique character, with a handle on each side formed as a drooping acanthus leaf. The foot is very simply moulded. Round the neck is another belt of classic foliation, with borders of leaves, flowers and ox-skulls, suspended by ribbons.

The style of this vase is good: and the ornaments are executed sharply and firmly, yet with great delicacy. It is of the best Florentine time, and might have been produced in the studio of Donatello. Or we may attribute it to Verrocchio, or one of his pupils. Verrocchio's works are by no means numerous, and are marked by great individuality and highly finished execution.

Bought for 206*l.*

I. 53

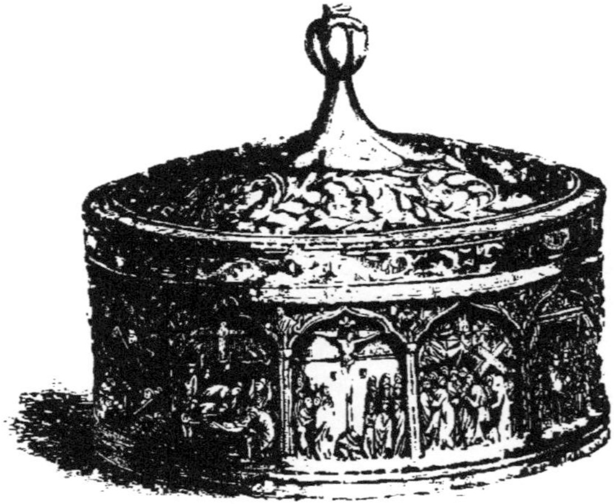

[illegible]

BOX.

B O X W O O D.

No. 1153—1864.

THIS box was intended and probably has been used for holding the unconsecrated wafers for mass. In this material, and of the same date, *i.e.* late in the fourteenth century, such examples are uncommon. It is possibly of Italian workmanship, and has been attributed to a Venetian artist. This, however, is very doubtful.

The decoration is rich, and the style and execution of the design are extremely good. The top is ornamented merely with foliated scroll work, with a plainer scroll on the flat silver mount below it. The body of the box is divided into twelve compartments with cusped arches over each, and a carved saint in high relief occupies every spandril. The subjects in the panels represent the different events of the Passion of our Lord; those which are shown in the etching being Pilate washing his hands, the carrying of the Cross, the Crucifixion, the Entombment, and the Resurrection. The figures filling the arches are something over half an inch in height. The etching is the full size of the original.

Bought for 16l.

I. 54

BRITANNIA . . . GREAT BRITAIN BRONZE . . . BRENT NIL . . . BRONZE
. . . BRONZE (SIGNED) . . . .
. . . .

INKSTAND.

BRONZE.

No. 575—1865.

THERE would be no impropriety in referring this fine inkstand to the studio of one of the pupils of Donatello, to Verrocchio, to Rustici, or Pollaiuolo, even if not to the great master himself. It is Florentine, of about the year 1470, excellently designed and executed with great care and completeness.

These remarks apply only to the inkstand itself; the cover and the figure of the Roman warrior at the top, although good and well modelled, are of later date; being north Italian, of the middle of the sixteenth century.

The inkstand is circular, in two stages, and supported on three feet in the form of antique masks, which rise above and spread over the lower divisions in double scrolls and leaf-work. Between these are other masks, with horns. On the upper stage garlands of flowers hang in pairs, suspended between three strapwork scrolls.

This example was formerly in the Soulages collection, and is about five inches high (without the cover) and six inches in width. A bronze candlestick in the Museum, No. 2089'55, is possibly by the same artist.

Bought for 20l.

JANVARY

DECORATIVE WALL

DECORATIVE WALL TILES.

JANUARY.

O NE of a series of large panels, representing the Seasons and the Months, which cover the upper portion of the walls of the grill room, or east dining room, in the South Kensington Museum. These panels are formed of glazed earthenware tiles, blue and white, with occasional touches of yellow.

All the decorations and fittings of this room are from the designs of Mr. E. J. Poynter, R.A. The tiles were painted from his drawings by female students of the South Kensington Museum porcelain class.

The dimensions of the panel represented are six feet two inches, by three feet seven inches.

CEILING   THE CERAMIC GALLERY

DESIGN:

FOR A CEILING.

O NE of the ceilings of two staircases leading to the lecture theatre at
the Museum. They were designed by Mr. F. W. Moody, instructor
in decorative art, and executed under his superintendence by two of his
pupils, Mr. W. Wise, and Mr. O. Gibbons.

The ceilings are painted in black and grey, with a few gold lines.

These staircases lead from the ceramic gallery; in which the various
panels of the roof are ornamented in a similar style; the designs, also by
Mr. Moody, being adapted to the form of the space to be covered.

FRIEZE DESIGNED BY GODFREY SYKES.

158

BOOK-COVER.

SILVER.

No. 2639—1855.

THIS is given as an example of a style of bookbinding, or rather of the decoration of the covers of a book, which during the last century has gone greatly out of fashion. As a mode of ornament, however, admitting much variety of detail from very simple to elaborate forms, it might be re-introduced with good effect.

The book-cover is probably Dutch, about the end of the seventeenth century, and the design consists of rich scrolls and foliage, twining and intertwisting in all directions, and enclosing birds. A space is left on the back for lettering, and the sides are hinged on to the back pieces. A couple of hinges close the book in front.

The size is about eight inches and a half by six and a half—sufficient for a large octavo volume.

Bought for 10*l.*

INKSTAND.

BRONZE.

No. 4673—1858.

A BEAUTIFUL example of a small inkstand in metal, imitating the shape so common about the same period for large chests. The model is rare, and the workmanship extremely good. It is Italian, of about the year 1520.

The cover is decorated in low relief with acanthus leaves and a grotesque mask, from which issue cornucopiæ. The sides have also in the centre a mask, connecting rich scrolls of foliated ornament which are continued to the corners. The stand rests upon four lions' feet. The interior of the lid has leafage, and a shield bearing two lions' paws erased, in saltire : these may be the arms of the Rasponi family of Ravenna who bore lions' paws azure, erased gules, on a golden field.

The inkstand is about nine inches long by nearly four high, and five inches wide ; it is in perfect condition, and no portion has been restored.

Bought for 16*l.*

I. 59

ROOD-CROSS IN SILVER PARCEL
GILT, WITH QUATREFOILS OF ENAMEL &
FIGURES OF THE V RGIN AND ST JOHN

GERMAN EARLY PART OF THE LF
.... IN SOLTYKOFF COLL.... PEN NO 251
J COLDALL FECIT

ROOD CROSS.

SILVER, PARCEL GILT.

No. 7939—1862.

THIS fine specimen of mediæval art in silver was formerly in the
famous Soltikoff collection, and combines several good examples of
more than one kind of work. The cross itself is set with quatrefoils of
enamel and pearls; on one side stands the blessed Virgin, and on the other
is St. John. The workmanship is German; and the date possibly about 1400;
but more probably some years later.

The cross is chased with a single reed moulding, forming as it were a
second and interior thin cross, and the figure of our Lord is fixed upon the
centre reed.   The ends are quatrefoils with quirks at the point of junction.
The quatrefoils are filled in with very richly coloured flowers in enamel, and
above the head of the cross the title INRI in gothic letters is also inscribed
upon a scroll in enamel.   Each quatrefoil, besides the enamelled flower, has
a smaller flower composed of seven pearls pierced and pinned to the surface.
The stem of the cross issues from a short stem terminating in a floriated
ornament, and this again grows from a larger flower of which the leaves
are serrated, curled, and turned in many directions.

Two richly decorated and curling leaf brackets spread immediately
below the cross, and at the extremities are placed, one on each side,
the figures of the Virgin and St. John.   The character and style of these
brackets induce the conclusion that the whole work should be attributed to
a later date than the year 1400.   The two figures stand on small enamelled
pedestals, springing from beaten foliage.   The blessed Virgin is vested
in a large mantle : a veil covering her head : she looks upward to the
cross with a look of anguish, and folds her hands one over another, in a
gesture of resignation.   The robe of St. John covers him also from head to
foot, his hair falls behind over his shoulders, and he clasps his hands before

I. 60

him. Very probably both these figures have been enamelled, but very slight, if any, traces now remain upon the silver.

Under the figures is a boss fluted down its surface with rows of beads on the projecting parts, having elegant scroll work on the edge connecting it with the base. The base expands in eight lobes below the boss, each lobe flat, but having a star and panel partly decorated with flowers. These panels have been filled with enamel of which the lines may still be distinguished ; but the enamel has entirely perished or been destroyed. The lobes project with eight semi-circles round the bottom moulding, which is graceful and executed with no less detail than the other portions. Eight projections of small quatrefoils are divided from each other by boldly designed thistle leaves.

It is greatly to be regretted that so much of the enamel of this piece of silversmiths' work has been lost. A great deal of the original splendour of the rood cross has, of course, been diminished. Nevertheless, the Museum contains few examples of German work so fine of the same period. The whole cross stands rather above one foot and a half in height.

Bought for 68l.

BOX.

THIS remarkable example of oriental art, executed during the occupation of part of Spain by the Moors, is of the tenth century; and not only to be admired for the beauty of its design and workmanship, but important as giving us the date at which it was made.

Spanish ivories of the middle ages, from the eighth to the fifteenth century, are extremely rare. The few which have been preserved (unlike the present specimen, which has an unmixed eastern style) still show almost always the influence of a Moorish or European feeling and purpose. Generally, also, they are either caskets or small boxes, which having found their way into the treasuries of Spanish churches are still preserved there. Some of the Spanish ivories are as old as the days of the Cordovan caliphs of the ninth century; and some in spite of their Arabic inscriptions, very commonly texts taken from the Koran and in honour of Allah, serve to contain relics of Christian saints. Probably this would not be, if the ecclesiastics to whose charge they are given could interpret the legends.

Another remarkable characteristic of the Spanish Moresque ivory boxes is that they often give, added to the inscription, the name of the artist. It is well known that very few names indeed are recorded of the innumerable sculptors of ivory diptychs and shrines, statuettes, caskets, mirror cases, combs, and all kinds of things, which for centuries were common in western Europe and in Italy. To these may now be added "Mohammed Ben Assarag," and "Mohammed Ibn Zeiyan," besides others who flourished in the eleventh century.

This box is carved throughout in open or pierced work, excepting the bottom of it. Narrow bands interlace, forming quatrefoils in which upon the cover are four eagles standing erect and with expanded wings. A small knob serves to lift the lid. Below the top of the cover is a band on which is an inscription, somewhat mutilated, giving the name of a caliph who reigned from A. D. 961 to 976. It reads, "A favour of God to the servant of God, al Hakem al Mostanser Billah, commander of the faithful."

The box has been at one time subjected to great heat or an accident by fire. The ivory has become fragile, like some of the famous Nineveh ivories, and should be very carefully handled. The etching gives the full size of the original.

Bought for 112*l.*

I. 61

PORTION OF THE SYON COPE.

PORTION OF THE SYON COPE.

NEEDLEWORK. No. 83—1864.

THERE are many very valuable and admirable pieces of mediæval
embroidery and needlework to be found in public museums or
ecclesiastical sacristies and treasuries in England and abroad. Some of
these are famous as examples of ancient art, like the Anglo-saxon stole
(so-called) of St. Cuthbert, in the cathedral library at Durham ; or
because of the renown or sanctity of the original owner, like the vestments
of St. Thomas à Becket at Sens ; or because of its historical importance,
like the celebrated tapestry of Bayeux. To these may be added " the Syon
Cope," of which a small portion is represented in the engraving. Splendid
as is the collection of textiles at South Kensington, this cope may be
regarded as the chief among them all, not merely on account of its early
date or good state of preservation or beauty of workmanship, but for the
skill displayed in designing the religious subjects upon it, and for the
numerous armorial bearings of great and historical English families with
which it is also decorated.

The history of this magnificent vestment is obscure. Nothing certain
about it is known, except that about sixty years ago it was brought back to
England from Lisbon, where it had been kept in the convent of the nuns
of St. Bridget. These nuns were the same community as that which,
originally founded by Henry the fifth in 1414, had flourished until the
reign of Henry the eighth at Syon, in Middlesex. There is every reason
to believe that the cope belonged to them from the time of their foundation
—a present probably for their chapel—and when their convent was
dissolved, and they were themselves driven out of England, the cope was
taken as one among the most prized of their possessions. During the
seventeenth and part of the eighteenth century the nuns, still keeping up
their ancient rule and sufficient numbers for community, resided first in
Flanders, then in France, and afterwards at Lisbon. Returning to
England, they brought the cope with them. Some years afterwards they
gave this vestment to John earl of Shrewsbury, who died in 1863, and
from his executors it was obtained for the Kensington Museum.

About the middle of the thirteenth century a new method of needlework
or embroidery was, as it seems, invented in England. Still retaining the
old " feather stitch " the needlewomen mixed it with a new style ; and so
greatly was this admired that it was commonly known and spoken of
abroad as " opus Anglicum," or English work. There is no better example
of this " opus Anglicum " extant than the Syon cope.

On careful examination the student will find that wherever the face or
other portion of the body is shown in any of the figures, the first stitches

were begun in the centre of the cheek and worked in circular lines ; falling
into straight lines again after the middle had been finished, and so carried
on through the rest of the fleshes. After the whole figure had thus been
wrought those portions of the face or parts which had been worked in
circular lines were pressed down with the small bulb or knob of an iron rod,
slightly heated. This is well seen also in the depression of the throat,
especially of an aged person. By the hollows thus lastingly sunk a play
of light and shadow is obtained, lending to the portion so treated a look
of being done in low relief. The figure of the Saviour on the cope is, as
usual in subjects of the crucifixion, but slightly clothed, and the "opus
Anglicum" may be studied in that part of the work.

It is not possible to show with any success at all in the illustration
the peculiarity of this beautiful kind of needlework ; nor has it been
attempted. But it has been somewhat less difficult with the groundwork
or filling in of the quatrefoils which, interlacing one another and enclosing
figures of our Lord and various saints, fill the whole vestment. This
groundwork is done in a long zigzag diaper pattern, after the fashion called
in ancient inventories "opus plumarium," from the way in which the
stitches overlie each other like the feathers on a bird.

The subjects on the cope are, beginning in the middle at the lowest
part, St. Michael overcoming Satan ; above this, the Crucifixion ; again, at
the top, the Saviour sitting on a throne in majesty. On the right of the
centre is the death of the blessed Virgin, upon the left is her burial. All
these are enclosed in cusped quatrefoils : and in other quatrefoils are eight
of the apostles. In its first and perfect state the cope had the whole
twelve : fragments of them still remain. It would seem that when the
orphrey and border containing the shields of arms were added the
lower part of the vestment was cut away. This was perhaps fifty years
after the centre of the cope was worked.

The figure represented in the engraving is St. Paul holding in one
hand his emblem, a sword, and in the other a closed book. A small portion
of the death of the Virgin is shown in the adjoining quatrefoil. The spaces
between the quatrefoils are filled with angels having, according to their
different hierarchies, two, four, or six wings.

The chief armorial bearings are those of Warwick, Ferrers, Clifford,
Spencer, Monteney, Percy, Bigod, Boteler, and Mortimer. Besides these,
Castile and Leon occurs more than once. It is by no means improbable
that Eleanor of Castile (queen of Edward the first), who died in 1290,
either ordered these additions to be made or herself took part in the
working of them.

The canvas for every part of the cope is of the very finest sort, and the
materials used are gold, silver, and various-coloured silks. It measures
nine feet seven inches by four feet three inches.

Bought for 110*l.*

GOBLET AGATE MOUNTED IN SILVER-GILT,   HALL MARKED ...
H 7½ IN DIA 3⅞ IN   B. K. M. (NO 38 67)   W M M gravit cit

163

CUP.

THE agate of which the cup is made is clouded in colour, although hollowed out very thin. It measures about three inches in depth, by three and five-eighths in diameter. The base is solid, resting on and inserted into the silver stand. Round the top is a rim of admirably adapted width, with a Vandyke-shaped ornament, thoroughly characteristic of the period when the cup was mounted.

The silver foot upon which the cup stands is very richly decorated; the large boss immediately beneath it with fruits, flowers, and lions' heads in very high relief, of excellent design and equally excellent workmanship. The different subjects are separated by flat narrow bands, dividing them into panels. This boss rests upon a small open-work table with four feet having each three claws, under which, again, is a half baluster-shaped support, also divided into panels filled with fruit ornaments. Below this, and separated only by a narrow rim which gives great variety to the design, the foot spreads in two divisions, the smaller above the larger. On the upper part are four snails issuing from their shells and creeping to the edge : on the lower are four dolphins, and between each of them is a crab.

No piece of English plate in the Museum excels this in quality of design and workmanship, nor in importance. It is Elizabethan and the hall mark is 1567. Nothing is known about the previous history of this beautiful cup, but some have suggested, and with a reasonable possibility, that it may have been mounted for some company of fishmongers, because of the dolphins and shell-fish on the base.

The cup is nearly eight inches in height.

Bought for 35ol.

PANDURINA.

BEECHWOOD.

No. 219—1866.

THIS musical instrument, somewhat resembling a lute in shape, is Italian and was made about the middle of the sixteenth century. The material is beechwood.

Various instruments of this kind were in common use in Europe during the middle ages, especially in Italy; and were known by the names also of *mandora*, *mandorina*, and *mandolino*. The mandora had usually for each tone two strings, catgut and wire; and there were eight pairs of them. The mandorina had four wire strings and resembled a diminutive lute, but its finger-board had metal frets, and the strings were fastened to little ivory pins at the end of the body instead of being looped through holes in the bridge. It differed from the pandurina chiefly in having a rounder and deeper body, and in having the tuning-pegs placed at the back of the head. The pandurina had a sort of scroll, with the tuning-pegs placed sideways as in the old English cither.

The present example is very richly carved, well designed, and well executed. Within a large cartouche in the centre are the three goddesses Juno, Minerva, and Venus, grouped somewhat after the manner of the Graces and as if waiting for the judgment of Paris. After the decision they would probably not have been seen standing together so amicably; and we remember no other occasion on which the three are said to have met in the same kind of way. But the part of Paris is left out. An ornamental composition of scroll and strap work with foliage surrounds the group of goddesses, completely filling the whole body of the instrument.

The stem is decorated with straight lines slightly designed, and terminates with a fine and bold head of Medusa. There are seven tuning-pegs, of which six are shown in the illustration.

The instrument measures nearly one foot five inches in length, and the width is four inches and a half.

Bought for 140*l*.

I. 64

DETAILS OF STAIRCASE DECORATION

DETAILS OF DECORATION.

PORTIONS of the decorations in enamelled terra cotta, ornamenting the west staircase leading to the ceramic gallery, are represented in this etching.

They were designed by Mr. Moody and executed by Messrs. Minton. The two larger panels are in Mr. Colin Minton's vitrified ceramic painting.

PANEL OF WINDOW FRAME, SOUTH KENSINGTON MUSEUM.
DESIGNED BY GODFREY SYKES.

1. 65

ANE ANT GESDEL MAGNIZ CERLERS BRONZ SAMMLUG

VASE AND COVER.

BRONZE.

No. 140—1865.

THIS bronze is not in good condition, having been cleaned overmuch and re-coloured. A very good judge, Mr. Drury Fortnum, expresses some doubt as to the genuineness of it; but, upon the whole, the evidence seems to be in its favour, although the ornamentation is somewhat exaggerated. The general style and modelling are not unworthy of examination, and portions of it might be adapted with advantage for small things in daily use.

The shape is elliptic, and the workmanship Italian, of the middle of the sixteenth century. On the cover is a boy, unclothed, who supports a shield bearing three fishes. The cover below the flat upon which the boy stands is divided into four panels, separated by projecting scrolls, and filled with figures representing harpies.

The top border is ornamented with well-designed acanthus leaves, beneath which is a receding band of oval divisions, in which are small dolphins. The lowest portion of the vase swells out again, having a series of gadroons of strapwork and four projecting heads of lions. The support below consists of four lions' feet.

The height is nearly ten inches, and the diameter eight inches.

Bought for 12l.

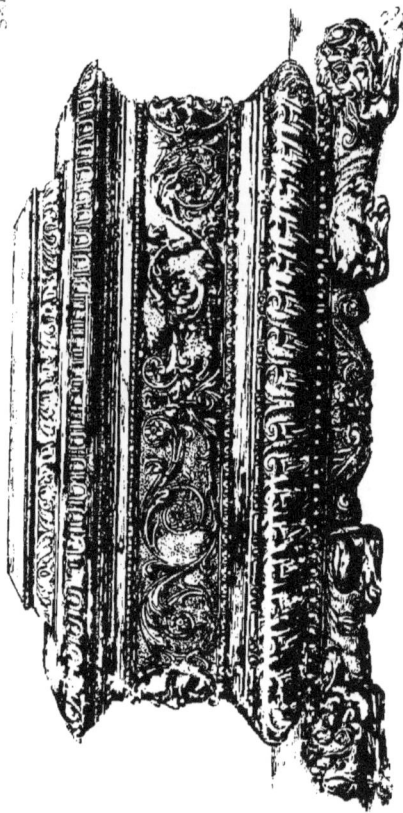

CHEST.

WALNUT WOOD.

THERE are few things still existing of the furniture of the fifteenth and sixteenth centuries more important and handsome than the Italian chests, coffers, or cassoni. The chest shown in the illustration is of a small size compared with many others, but is equally useful as exhibiting the usual style and mode of ornamentation.

The larger-sized chests, of which there are several magnificent examples in the South Kensington Museum, were the most striking as well as the chief pieces of furniture in the rooms of the mediæval Italian palaces. In fact, with the exception of some chairs and perhaps a great table, there was little else. They were placed often along the halls and corridors; and were designed, carved, and painted or gilded in accordance with the architectural details of the building. They were used for containing clothes, or ornamental hangings, and rich stuffs. A not uncommon material for them was a kind of cypress, which has a strong aromatic and very pleasant scent and keeps off moths. Chests, however, made of this kind of wood are altogether different in the style of decoration from the more common cassoni. They are made almost always without mouldings, or with very slight mouldings; and the ornaments consist not of carved work, but of subjects or patterns etched or lined in with a pen, or sometimes incised, and the intervals worked over with punches, and occasionally filled in with black pigment.

Chests of a large size were frequently made in pairs; sometimes also they formed parts of long sets, fours or sixes, according as they were intended for the wall spaces of galleries or rooms, or for portions of walls between doors. Very frequently also the carvings were helped out with gilding. Boxes or coffers of the size of the present specimen were usually bridal presents; and they vary so much as to be occasionally intended evidently to hold scarcely anything but jewels and small ornaments. But

I. 67

these even still retain in little all the features and large style of the big cassoni.

This box is of about the middle of the sixteenth century, carved in walnut wood. The lid shuts on a bold cornice moulding, and rises above into a central solid panel. The front panel is filled with an admirably designed scroll of foliage in the middle of which, under the keyhole, is a bold mask. Other masks are placed at the corners. Underneath is a projecting base cut into gadroons or flutings or ribs alternately. The contrast of the richly carved portions with the lines of moulding broadest and most spreading at the base, and gradually shorter as the composition rises, gives great effect to the whole.

The support of the box consists of crouching lions, united in the middle by a couple of scrolls between which is another mask.

Italian mediæval chests, and also of the renaissance, were not uncommonly to be obtained for moderate prices twenty or thirty years ago. They have, since, become very scarce and very dear. Large and handsome examples fetch extremely high prices ; and, in fact, it would be now almost impossible to gather together again such a collection as that possessed by the South Kensington Museum.

This box or casket measures in height one foot four inches, in length two feet eight, and in width one foot three inches.

Bought for 10*l.*

SILVER HANDLED KNIFE

ASCRIBED TO POLLAJUOLO, ITALIAN ABOUT 1475   S.K.M. (no 2484) JOHN S. COMYNS, 18..?

KNIFE.

STEEL AND SILVER.

No. 7525—1859.

POLLAIUOLO, to whom this knife (or rather the handle) has been ascribed, was born in 1454 and died in 1509. He is chiefly known by his works in bronze although, like most of the bronzists of his time, he was also a goldsmith, a painter, and a niellist. Pollaiuolo was taught in the school of Ghiberti, and the beautiful frieze which surrounds Andrea Pisano's gate is chiefly ascribed to him. He executed also some of the subjects in relief upon the silver altar - frontal for the baptistery at Florence.

The knife-handle, which is silver, is divided into small panels, four on each of the two broader sides. The narrower sides are decorated with a floriated ornament running the whole length.

The panels on one side are filled with a procession of horse and foot soldiers ; the smallest of them has a group of four soldiers surrounding a shield on which is represented a tree with spreading branches. The subjects on the opposite side are the Judgment of Paris, and the Judgment of Solomon, with two others not easily to be understood. This may seem a curious mixture, but not more so than the collections of tales and legends in the fifteenth and sixteenth centuries ; as, for example, in a book then universally read in almost every European country, the *Gesta Romanorum*.

The flat band and bracket at the top have been gilded.

Bought for 60*l.*

INKSTAND.

BRONZE.

No. 2089—1855.

CIRCULAR in shape, this Italian inkstand is admirable in design. Formerly it was in the Bernal collection ; and may be compared with another inkstand also in the Museum, No. 575 '65, and with the candlestick, No. 552 '65. We can have little doubt that they all came from the same studio, if not absolutely modelled by the hand of the same artist. It is well worthy of careful study. The graduation of the outlines and the judicious application and arrangement of the ornaments combine well with the supporting terminal feet. The cover is unfortunately wanting.

Formed in two stages, the upper one rests upon the heads of three satyrs, whose feet, ending as floriated terminals, support the base. Masks, alternating with shells and seated lions, ornament the moulding immediately below the cover. The under part, which is of double width, is enriched between each supporting satyr with masks in high relief, and with very elegantly disposed scrolls running along the whole surface. The etching is about the same size as the original.

Bought for 15l. 5s.

LAVRENTII · KYLIANI · GEORGII · OSWALDI
SEBASTIANI · MAVRITII · TEB · ... DIONISII · GREGORII · NICOLAI ·
S. PETRUS · PANCRATII
S. FAUSTIN
SIPLICII
S. BONIFACII · PAULUS

PORTABLE ALTAR.

PORPHYRY.

No. 10—1873.

PORTABLE altars, dating from the middle ages, are of extreme rarity. They were not often of materials so valuable, nor enriched with so many decorations, as is the present example ; therefore, when worn out they were generally destroyed, and this with much care : because being consecrated and having relics inserted in the middle it would have been highly irreverent to leave them exposed to all kinds of accidents.

Their use for many centuries, and probably from very primitive times, has been universal in the Catholic Church. Priests who had distant missions, or who were sent for a short time only to places where there was no church or chapel with a consecrated altar, carried with them these portable altars, which could be placed upon any stand or table sufficiently decent and suitable. Notices of them are to be found in English records and inventories as far back as the eighth and ninth centuries.

This altar is German work of the twelfth century. The slab is porphyry, set in wood, plated over with thin gilt metal, plain on the edges but forming on the upper surface a double border of leaf-moulding, in the Rhenish-Byzantine style of the period. The front and the under sides round the edges are covered with figures and demi-figures of saints.

The slab has in the centre a crucifix ; our Saviour being represented with His feet nailed separately, and with a wide garment covering Him from the waist to the knees. Above His head is (unusual upon a crucifix) the symbolic emblem of the Father and the Holy Spirit, forming with our Lord the Three Persons of the Trinity. The Eternal Father, with hands extended, supports the arms of the cross, and the mystic Dove descends upon the Saviour's head.

Four full-length figures stand by the cross, two on either side. Upon the right of it St. Boniface and St. Paul, the one holding a pastoral staff, the other a book, and both pointing to the crucifix. On the other side are

I. 70

St. Peter and St. Pancratius : in the hand of the first are the keys, and St. Pancratius has a palm-branch. The names of the four saints are inscribed above their heads.

Two demi-figures of saints in armour, and holding shields and swords, are in circles placed at the foot of the cross. The fashion of the shields and of the helmets would lead to the conclusion that this altar was made very early in the twelfth century, of which the style of the letters of the inscriptions is a further evidence. St. Simplicius and St. Faustinus are the two saints within the circles.

Two mouldings of different patterns surround the crucifix and figures. These are separated by a plain band carrying a longer inscription explaining that relics, not only of these six saints, are inserted in the altar-stone, but also those of St. Laurence, St. Oswald, and several others. Relics are a necessary part of, and must be enclosed in, every altar or altar-stone according to the ritual of the Catholic Church.

The under part of the altar-stone is also decorated with compositions representing the Nativity, the Crucifixion, the Resurrection, and the Ascension. There are also several inscriptions.

This slab came from the collection of the bishop of Hildesheim. The length is rather more than fifteen inches, by nine in width.

CUP.

SILVER: GILT.

No. 485—1873.

A CUP of Augsburg work, made about the end of the sixteenth century. The mouth is cylindrical, with a diameter considerably less than that of the body, which is acorn-shaped, having the widest part uppermost. The upper portion of the cup, where the diameter is largest, is filled with oval medallions separated from each other by a rich foliated ornament; three of these contain heads, finely designed, two of which are female. Below this comes a plain moulding, recessed : and again, below, the bottom of the cup has oval medallions repeated with a rich strap decoration between them.

The stem has a bold knop ornamented with foliage, rams' heads, and scrolls. From this spring three slight and elegant brackets, with cupids' heads on them and winged below, supporting the cup. The surfaces of the stem and foot are beaten and chased with masks, arabesques, and grotesques. Much additional splendour is also given by the judicious distribution of the oval medallions, most of which remain polished and luminous in contrast with the delicate reliefs and lines of the rest of the decoration.

The shape and arrangement of the mouth show that the cup has been double ; the two mouths fitting one into the other. It measures about eight inches and a half in height, with a diameter of four inches and a half. The cup came from the Webb collection, and the workmanship as well as the design is extremely good.

Bought for 130*l.*

MIRROR FRAME.

I·72

DESIGN FOR A MIRROR-FRAME,

OR FOR A PANEL.

No. 2327.   Art Library.

A DRAWING, pen and sepia on paper, which is ascribed to Pierino del Vaga.   The two sides are different, and rather roughly carried out—indeed, so carelessly that the design leans to one side.   But it is full of suggestions which may be useful to art workmen and to students.

A small sketch of a candelabrum fills the space on the right side : a terminal figure occupies, as a decoration, the corresponding space upon the left.

ONE BAY OF WATER COLOUR GALLERIE

F. REDGRAVE R.A INV

W. REID JNR

DESIGN.

ONE BAY OF THE WATER-COLOUR GALLERIES.

GALLERIES arranged for the exhibition of the very important and large collection of water-colour drawings belonging to the Museum were opened in 1862. The general decorations of the walls, pilasters, cornices, &c., were designed by R. Redgrave, R.A., at that time inspector-general for art. The lunette in the bay shown in the engraving is also from his design, and was painted by R. C. Puckett.

There are eighteen side bays, each containing an oil painting in the lunette. Several of these are by well-known artists—by Leslie, Marks, Eyre Crowe, Yeames, and others.

FRIEZE IN REFRESHMENT ROOM, SOUTH KENSINGTON MUSEUM, DESIGNED BY J. GAMBLE.

PYX.

SILVER GILT.

No. 4689—1858.

THE greater number of pieces of plate whether of English or of foreign work of the middle ages which have been preserved to our own time were originally made for ecclesiastical and not for secular use. This is a very natural consequence of the lapse of years. As people in private station succeeded each other there was often a disposition, independently of any other necessities, to get rid of things which had belonged to their predecessors : and precious metal when sold generally found its way to the melting-pot. Even changes of fashion had the same powerful influence then as now: and new owners in the days of queen Elizabeth or king James the first fancied the best work of the early part of the sixteenth century to be already out of date and old-fashioned. So the old was parted with and destroyed to obtain something new.

There was a better chance for ecclesiastical plate : which in England, as we well know, suffered chiefly from the wholesale plundering in the reigns of Henry the eighth and Edward the sixth. Abroad, we must attribute to the frequent wars, and in later times to the French revolution, the loss of mediæval plate and ornaments. Happily, there still exist upon the continent many treasuries of churches and monasteries, in which may be found superb pieces of work in gold and silver, which have been carefully preserved by the several communities from generation to generation for hundreds of years.

This pyx is probably Flemish, of about the beginning of the fifteenth century. The general design is an elegant imitation of the lantern of a church tower. Hexagonal in shape, each side is divided by a buttress which rises with a lofty pinnacle above the wall which it supports. The lower portion of the buttress is pierced, giving the appearance of greater lightness, and the pinnacle ends with a small finial. A rich battlement runs along the top of the sides.

The panel in each side is filled with a figure, chased, and standing under a broad arch with cusps. In one panel is our Lord, holding an orb in one hand, and giving benediction with the other. In the other five are —1. St. John the baptist and the typical Lamb; 2. St. Matthew; 3. St. Catherine of Alexandria; 4. St. Ursula covering the multitude of virgins with her cloak; 5. An unknown saint, without an emblem.

Above the body of the pyx the roof slopes to a central shrine which also has light open-worked buttresses, to which the outside set as they rise up connect themselves by means of flying buttresses. The whole of this portion forms an open canopy, above which again (as a roof) rises a spire, crocketed at the angles and surmounted by a somewhat bolder finial and a cross. Beneath the canopy a small rectangular stand is placed, decorated with rows to imitate windows and with quatrefoils, which serves as a pedestal for a little image (of excellent design and execution) of the blessed Virgin and Child.

The stem is more plain in design; also six-sided; expanding immediately below the pyx in order to support it, and again considerably wider at the foot. In the middle is a boss or knop, more richly ornamented; intended to assist in holding the pyx in the same way as in the case of a chalice. Round the knop are six quatrefoils in lozenge plaques. The foot spreads into six semicircular lobes, having a moulded edge with fine leaf-work upon it.

The height of this pyx is nineteen inches, and the diameter seven.

Bought for 45l.

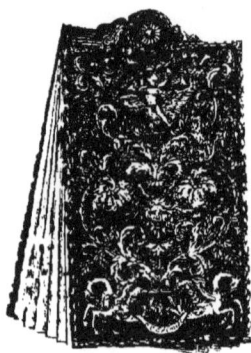

C TAH ETA VINU EAVES S VIL
VIA   GERMAN CAR   n

WRITING TABLETS.

IVORY AND SILVER.

No. 299—1854.

THE leaves of these tablets are ivory, and the cover is silver gilt. Not much, of course, can be learnt from the leaves which are thin and smooth, as in all tablets of this kind. But the cover is very elegantly designed and well executed; the date about 1740.

Although this example is in silver, the same ornament and decoration would look admirably well carved in ivory. It consists of delicately formed scrolls of branches and foliage, repeated on each side. At the top a small cupid rides upon an eagle, and the centre has a mask or lion's head, below which are two grotesque animals from whose bodies the scrolls spring and extend upwards.

The sculpture is signed with a German name, Schmide; but the design is either Italian or French, more probably the latter. The tablets measure three inches by one and three-quarters.

Bought for 15*l.*

CHEST.

OAK.

No. 6746—1859.

A GOOD example of a mediæval chest, in a style which may be attributed
rather to England than to France or Flanders. There is much in
the design and execution which would lead to the opinion that it is English
work : and very possibly it was originally made for some church purpose,
to hold vestments, or books, or records.

The date is about the middle of the fifteenth century. It is a chest
of which the side frame-pieces are prolonged into legs. There is a bar
ornamented with a rich scroll of foliage, below the panels in front. The
sides have the well-known "linen" pattern, at that time becoming common;
and on each door is a mask in relief. The front has also open work,
flamboyant tracery in two narrow panels; evidently introduced for the
purpose of ventilating the interior. The chest stands about three
feet high.

Bought for 3l. 4s.

TRIPTYCH.

IVORY.

No. 4336—1857.

TRIPTYCHS of this style and period, early in the sixteenth century, are extremely rare; it is possible that they were made at that time, but nevertheless they seem to have been destroyed more frequently than older ones, or were less valued and therefore less taken care of. It is possible also that the fashion of this kind of devotional tablets, either for churches or for private use, was gradually dying out; as, in fact, we know that comparatively very few diptychs or triptychs are now carved in ivory.

The present example is French, of the early part of the sixteenth century. Evidently it was originally intended to hold a relic; and the design and execution are equally good.

The centre panel is filled with two angels, standing under an arch which has floriated cusps; they hold, each of them with both hands, a circle in which the relic was, of course, to be placed. This has been removed or lost. The angels are clothed in long robes, reaching to the feet; and a tunic with sleeves half-way down the arm is again worn over the vestment. Their heads are bound with a narrow fillet, from which the curls escape below. One wing of each angel is drawn in close, following the perpendicular line of the border; the other wing is raised and spread widely open, forming a background to the head and following the upward inside curve of the arch.

The background of the centre and of both wings is richly decorated with bold fleurs-de-lis, and the intermediate spaces are diapered with delicately drawn crossed lines. The whole, figures and ornamental details, is carved in low but effective relief.

In height the centre-piece measures eight inches and a quarter; in width five inches. The width of each wing is two inches and a half.

Bought for 20l.

I. 77

BECHER UND DECKELPOKAL
SILBER, GETRIEBEN, VERGOLDET
XVI. JAHRHUNDERT

CUPS.

SILVER.

No. 4688—1858, and No. 9016—1863.

BOTH are German work and of about the same date, late in the six-teenth century. The cup to the left, lying on its side, is rather the earliest. They are useful examples of the style of that period.

The mouth of the left hand cup is slightly bell-shaped; and is orna-mented under the lip with delicate engraving collected in masses of strap-work with heads introduced. Somewhat more than half-way down (at the smallest diameter) is a cord moulding, dividing the cup. The lower part is filled with two rows of round growing seeds pierced by a point; the flat spaces between are decorated with a slightly incised small leaf ornament, very commonly found in English plate of the time of queen Elizabeth. A row of balls, alternately with the points of the semicircles in which the balls are set, surrounds the base. The cup stands about five inches high.

The other, the upright cup, is overlaid with scroll ornament, beaten up on the sides; the shape is not good but characteristic. Small plates are attached to a rim by links a little below the mouth. This cup is nearly five inches in height.

Bought for 6l. 10s. and 1l. 12s.

VENETIAN GLASS BEAKER 5954-'58.

379

BEAKER AND COVER.

GLASS.

No. 5954—1858.

A N example of Venetian manufacture of the beginning of the sixteenth
century, and highly characteristic of the period when it was made.
The glass is clear, with transverse fillets forming a somewhat wide band
in the middle, decorated with six masks and rose ornaments. Three of
each of these are on the cover; three on the central band. These are
moulded and gilt. Below is a gadroon-shaped edging immediately above
the support, which is formed of three round balls, also gilded.

This beaker was probably made at Murano where the chief Venetian
glass-houses were established, at the time when the workshops there
began to produce vases, cups, and plates of far better design and quality
than those of an earlier period. It is to about the end of the fifteenth and
the beginning of the sixteenth century that we must especially ascribe
those glass vessels of almost every shape and kind, and of most fragile
quality, whose elegant forms have ever made them admired by all who
have a true feeling for beauty, and which bespeak the artist rather than
the artisan.

This beaker measures eight inches in height, with a diameter of three
inches and a quarter.

Bought for 10*l.*

I-80

MORSE.

SILVER GILT.

No. 394—1872.

THE morses or clasps by which in the middle ages the heavy vestments of ecclesiastics were fastened together were often very richly ornamented, and generally with conventional designs. But the example shown in the illustration is unusually rich, and represents in relief upon enamel more than one scriptural subject.

The whole morse is silver gilded in parts and surrounded by a border sloping inwards, covered with vine stems and leaves in relief, all well carried out in the details. Among the leaves are set eight small pearls, and the outer rim is finished with a cord moulding.

Inside the border the morse is filled with blue translucent enamel, forming a background upon which is displayed an architectural frontispiece in several stories and of elaborate design. The lowest of these consists of an arcade filled with pointed arches, like the side of a cloister. The extremities of the arcade come forward in two blocks, showing three sides of an octagon termination. The centre, in consequence of this arrangement, forms a recess; and in this is a representation of the Adoration of the Magi. St. Joseph is not shown; and the blessed Virgin seated holds the infant Saviour on her knees. One of the magi stands behind, clothed in a long robe; a second kneels before our Lord, offering Him a cup of gold; and the third appears waiting at the entrance, which seems to be a square-headed doorway, and holds his cap in his hand.

The next stage above is backed by another richly decorated façade; in the middle are two small figures standing in a deep recess under a canopy of two arches. They may be two spectators, but two other figures on the same platform have been interpreted as representing Herod and a soldier (who has a drawn sword over his shoulder) to whom he is giving orders.

Again, above all, is a third stage or story with turrets and parapet with battlements. In the centre is another widely open canopy, at the extremities of which stand two other figures who have been supposed to represent Joachim and Anna.

The two sides of the central portion are carried up to unequal heights, and in two different designs. They balance one another; and the artist may have wished to represent some existing building which he was familiar with or have taken a pleasure in varying the architectural details of this elaborate front.

Below the chief subject is a division of which the background is filled with green enamel, intended to represent a sloping mountain. On the midst of it stands the holy house of Loreto, a small building of one room, with an arched door, a window, and a dormer window in the roof. Outside, the blessed Virgin (shown of a size far too large to pass into the house) is seen sitting and reading. There are also a lily, a dog, a hare, a knight, and flowers scattered over the hill. The whole subject is carved and chased upon a very minute scale, the house being scarcely three quarters of an inch in height.

This very curious morse is remarkable for the admirable skill shown in the workmanship. The architecture is full of quaint details which are only to be recognized on a careful study of the metal work itself. Small as the scale is, every portion is made out with astonishing correctness.

The work is probably German, of about the middle of the fifteenth century. The diameter is five inches.

Bought for 350*l.*

BERGHAMS GALLERY

INTERIOR OF THE SHEEPSHANKS
GALLERY.

ONE of the galleries containing the collection of pictures by British artists, bequeathed in the year 1857 to the South Kensington Museum by Mr. Sheepshanks. The galleries were opened in 1865. Captain Fowke, R.E., supplied the designs for the buildings and Godfrey Sykes for the decorations.

One of the conditions under Mr. Sheepshanks' will was that the collection should be exhibited in a suitable and well-lighted gallery, to be called "The National Gallery of British Art," at South Kensington. It is among the most important collections of pictures by British artists, and at Mr. Sheepshanks' death was valued at £53,000 ; at the present time worth a much larger sum.

When first received at the Museum the collection was exhibited for a few years in some small rooms, which now serve for other purposes.

DAGGER-SHEATH, AND HILT.

IVORY.

No. 147—1866.

A VERY rare example of what must have been, in the middle ages, a somewhat large class of works in ivory. Few things were better adapted to the peculiar form of the tusk, than the knives and daggers of that period. Common, however, sheaths could not have been ; the cost of the material must always have limited the use of them to wealthy people.

The work is Italian, of the fourteenth century ; and the length altogether is nearly fifteen inches.

The top of the hilt is carved with a crouching lion in high relief, under open work to represent branches of trees which spring from a trunk on each side and meet over his back. One side of the hilt has a nondescript and grotesque-looking animal, with the head of a dragon and the wings and legs of a bird : the other side, a female centaur with a lute. These are surrounded with foliated branches, also in pierced or open work. Under them is a narrow band ornamented with rabbits or hares.

The sheath is quite plain on one side. The other is divided into two unequal compartments. In the upper is a gentleman kneeling before a lady, who holds a dog in her lap. He is dressed in a loose robe with a hood ; the lady in a long gown with a border round the bodice. This subject is in the same style and manner as the decorations of the caskets, combs, and mirror cases of the same period. The lower compartment has two curious-looking animals, placed back to back ; one like a lion, the other like a bird, with their tails carried on to the point in interlacing scrolls.

The sheath and hilt have been originally coloured and gilt, traces of which still remain.

Bought for 140*l.*

:. 82

HAND BELL BRONZE (SOULAGES COLL) ITALIAN DATE ABOUT 1500
S.K.M. (No 587.85.) M.G. MACKANESS ETC.Y

344

HAND BELL.

BRONZE.

No. 587—1865.

THIS bell, of Italian design and workmanship early in the sixteenth
century, was formerly in the Soulages collection. The decoration
round the body of the bell consists of wreaths of flowers suspended from
masks, having above on a band the words *Pulsv. meo. servs. voco. lipo.
mano. tvos.* Between the wreaths are profile heads and a shield of arms.
The shield bears a bend between two tigers' heads. The mouth of the bell
has a wide border ; richly filled with acanthus leaves.

Inside, in relief, is a mark ⚔ probably that of the founder.

A somewhat similar bell and of about the same period is in the
Museum, No. 586 '65. Also from the Soulages collection.

Bought for 3l.

I. 83

CROSIER
IN GILT METAL ENAMELLED
ITALIAN 13 CENTURY
S K M (4p 7931/JAD CAMPBELL, DEC

PASTORAL STAFF.

METAL GILT.

No. 7951—1862.

ONE or two examples of crosiers or pastoral staffs made of ivory have already been given in this series ; another material, more common in the middle ages and admitting a great variety of decorations, was metal. This was often enamelled and almost always gilded. Occasionally, also, gems and uncut stones or crystals were inserted in the volute.

The staff shown in the illustration is of a rather unusual form, having a plainly-shaped round cross-piece at the top of the staff. The staff or stem itself is round, but the curve is four-sided in section with a delicate cresting on the outside.

The ornamentation is translucent enamel on silver. Diamond-shaped divisions fill the stem, in quatrefoils applied in separate plates and joined at the points with flowers of beaten work, and each figure varied in design. The knop or cross-piece has six quatrefoil plaques on the circumference and ends, each filled with the half-figure of a saint; all in translucent enamel. They are the blessed Virgin and Child, St. Peter, St. Paul, St. Matthew, St. Romuald, and St. Maur.

The volute is, as has already been remarked, four-sided or lozenge-shaped. The diamond plaques of translucent enamel are continued up the curve, with half-diamonds ornamented with trefoils occupying the vacant spaces. The curve ends in a flat base or pedestal, on which is a figure of the blessed Virgin seated upon a throne, architecturally arcaded, and holding the infant Saviour, standing upright and embracing her, upon her knees. Kneeling before them, with hands raised in prayer or adoration, is a third figure vested as an abbot or a monk. Very probably this pastoral staff was made for the abbot of some mitred monastery. The whole group is well designed and of careful workmanship.

The volute is further enriched by two fine beaded bands running along the inside and outside borders ; and three boldly-designed floriated ornaments fill a broad moulding under the cross-piece which divides the crook from the staff.

This splendid crosier came from the Soltikoff collection, dispersed in 1862. It is Italian, of the fourteenth century. The length is twelve and a half inches, and the width of the curve five inches.

Bought for 241l.

I. 84

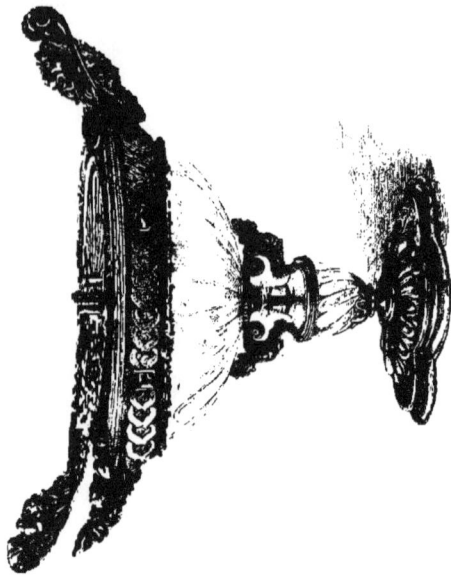

INCENSE-HOLDER OR BOAT.

SILVER AND CRYSTAL.

No. 1129—1864.

A GOOD example of this class of church utensils in the Italian style of the sixteenth century. The ship or boat itself is rock crystal, and the mount is silver-gilt. A small vial shaped crystal vase forms also a portion of the stem.

Round the rim is a band of guilloche chasing set with jewels. The lid is in two halves jointed and hinged in the middle, with handles ending, above and below, in admirably designed satyr masks in very bold relief. A legend runs round the cover, "*Dirigatur sicut incensum oratio mea. Psal.* 140." The foot is gadrooned, with a broad flat spreading base. The original is five inches high, and seven long; somewhat larger than it is shown in the etching.

The spoon by the side is not an ecclesiastical spoon: but also of about the same date and Italian workmanship. It is shell-shaped, with a terminal figure for a handle.

Bought for 85*l.*

I. 85

FOLDING-CHAIR.

WALNUT-WOOD.

No. 8123—1863.

A CHAIR of Flemish work, of the early part of the sixteenth century. It would be an useful pattern for modern use as a travelling-chair.

It is a child's chair made in the fashion of the camp chairs now common, the four legs formed of four pieces crossed from side to back like the letter X, and held in place by a piece of stuff or velvet that supplies also the seat. The back is merely the prolonged fore-legs, raking backwards; at the top they are joined and kept firm by a wide piece carved with arabesque foliage in relief. Two other bars are below, the centre one having a row of little arches; and the three are united by a series of small turned balusters in ebonized wood. The back and the bars connecting the legs are also carved in low relief.

The chair stands two feet and one inch high, by nearly fifteen inches wide.

Bought for 4l.

ABBILDUNG 11 CANDELABRUM STÜCK

PEDESTAL.

BRONZE.

No. 568—1865.

THIS is a very beautiful object, and reasonably believed to be modelled after a design by Donatello. It is of the best period of Florentine art in the fifteenth century. One of the highest authorities, Mr. J. C. Robinson, has no hesitation in saying that it can scarcely be the work of a less powerful hand than Donatello's.

The shape is quadrangular, and the panels contain alternately figures of fauns and bacchantes. The attitudes are varied, but all are full of energy and vigour. A delicate upright ornament of flowers fills small panels where the corners are cut away, and a bold scroll occupies the lowest moulding at the foot. The sentiment of the design is clearly derived from the antique, rendered in the masterly but characteristic style of the last half of the fifteenth century. Some similar examples are known : one, in the possession of Mr. Fortnum. This came to the Museum with the Soulages collection.

The illustration is of the full size of the original.

Bought for 10l.

E W E R.

PEWTER.

No. 4289—1857.

A GOOD example of the art of François Briot, of whose existing works almost every one which is known is in pewter. The material on which he employed himself was far less costly than what his excellence, both in design and execution, fairly deserved; and he spent upon pewter the same labour and showed the same skill as other artists have on cups, vases, and ewers of gold and silver.

The decoration of this ewer is in low relief. Under the lip—not shown in the illustration—is a clever and spirited mask. The body of the vase is divided into three compartments by horizontal bands, of which the upper is filled with winged horses and heads within circles. The middle has three oval cartouches; in each is a female figure, one with an anchor, another with children, and the third standing. The lowest border has grotesque figures sitting or squatting, with wings.

The handle has a female figure carved and lying on her back, shown undraped to the waist.

This ewer is marked in two places with the monogram FB.

Very little is told us of the history of François Briot. He worked during the reign of Henry II. of France (1547—1559). His best pieces are stamped with his name or mark; and the same character and style and shape are to be seen in all which are known. It has been said that a silver ewer of Briot's workmanship was melted down at the mint at Rouen in 1820.

The height of the present example is eleven inches by nearly five in width.

Bought for 5l. 10s.

ALPHABET DESIGNED BY GODFREY SYKE

ALPHABET.

DESIGNED BY GODFREY SYKES.

THESE letters appear frequently among the decorations of the Museum buildings, especially in the refreshment rooms and the ceramic gallery, where long inscriptions in glazed terra cotta form ornamental friezes.

They have also been used as initial letters in various publications relating to the Museum.

COCOA NUT.

MOUNTED IN SILVER.

No. 2116—1855.

A GOOD example of the German style of mounting a cocoa nut about the end of the sixteenth century, at that time a very common object for decoration not only abroad but in England. The fashion seems to have lasted for about sixty or eighty years. Examples are rare before 1550 and after 1620. Sometimes, in fact probably in the majority of such ornaments, the cup had a cover, which has often been lost or destroyed. The present specimen never had a cover.

The upper portion of the mount consists of a broad well-designed band of silver, divided into three narrower bands by delicately worked rims. The top band immediately under the mouth of the cup is incised with a running scroll pattern, in the midst of which within a circle is the date, 1585; an addition which gives great importance to the example. Below this is a narrower band filled with small figures, scrolls, and foliage. The lowest is more richly decorated and embossed with masks, heads, and panels in strap work. A vandyke-shaped border falls below this, clipping the cocoa nut.

The nut itself is clasped tightly by bands fastened to the mount above and below, by hinges, and ornamented with a vandyke edging. Where they intersect, pieces of malachite are inserted in small bosses. The centre of each compartment is filled with a lion's head, with a ring suspended from the mouth. These heads are characteristic of German work 'of that period; being over-ornamented with a meaningless decoration. English work, on a cup of the same date and in the same style, would have been much more simple and in better taste.

Slight and well-designed brackets support the bottom of the cup and rest upon the boss which swells from the middle of the stem. This boss is decorated with three lions' heads, two female heads, and one smaller head.

The foot is sufficiently enriched with small panels in strap work, with heads and masks, and fruit and foliage.

The nut itself has been left rough; giving, unfortunately, to the whole a somewhat unfinished and coarse appearance. The height is rather over eight inches, and the diameter four inches.

Bought for 46l.

I. 90

RELIQUARY.

CRYSTAL AND SILVER.

No. 4687—1858.

IT is extremely difficult to decide as to the country to which we can refer the workmanship of this remarkable reliquary. The design is unusual; two architectural ends supporting a polygonal crystal vase, the whole placed upon four columns. The date is undeniably about the middle of the fourteenth century : and whilst there seems to be very little in favour of the opinion (suggested by some) that it is Italian work, there is a good deal which supports the argument of those who would give it either to France or England. It is not wise to decide upon doubtful pieces of this character and date by hurriedly saying at once that they must be French. There were as many and as good artists in England as in France in mediæval days; and although it is true that by far the larger number of such works have been destroyed, yet occasionally some have been preserved to whose claims as being of English origin we may not unreasonably listen.

The ends of the framework contain each two panels under gables which surmount cusped arches, and are supported by buttresses with plain and rather heavy pinnacles. The panels are filled with four figures in high relief, the back and the front forming two subjects. They represent the blessed Virgin, St. Joseph, and two angels. Two of them were without doubt intended for a composition of the Annunciation, and two probably for the warning given to St. Joseph in the dream. The blessed Virgin is kneeling on one knee.

The reliquary stands on four columns, with capitals and other architectural details. They are fixed on a square base, in the middle of which is a round medallion containing a floriated ornament made by four intersecting semicircles, with trefoils of white on a green ground in champlevé enamel.

The crystal vase is polygonal and is kept horizontally in place by two mountings, one at each end. A band also runs along the top above the cylinder, ending with the centre pinnacles and connecting the ends firmly together. This is finished with a pierced cresting of fleurs-de-lis.

The reliquary stands about six inches and a half high; in fact, is rather larger and higher than the etching.

Bought for 40*l.*

I. 91

LAMP OR CANDLESTICK
BRONZE, ITALIAN,
ABOUT 1570. H. 14 INCHES.
SOULAGES COLLECTION.
S.K.M. No. 14.
W. WYATT F. XLI.

192

LAMP.

BRONZE.

No. 564—1865.

THIS bronze was formerly in the Soulages collection, and the lower portion is well worth careful study. It is made up of two separate pieces: the stand itself was originally in all probability a candlestick, into which a lamp has been afterwards inserted. Both are of Italian workmanship and somewhat late in the sixteenth century.

The stand, from which the nozzle of the candlestick has been removed and lost, consists of a pedestal having three feet; female figures terminating in foliating scrolls and connected together by boldly designed foliage. They support a small flat table on which a vase-shaped stem rests, decorated with whole-length figures alternating with the heads of goats. The lamp, which was originally made to be suspended, is in the form of a grotesque siren or mermaid whose tail is curled in the shape of the letter S, rising above her head.

The height is fourteen inches.

Bought for 18*l.*

I. 92

193

CRUCIFIX.

CEDAR, GOLD AND FILIGREE, AND IVORY.

No. 7943—1862.

F EW pieces of ecclesiastical metal work in the Museum have a richer and more precious appearance than this crucifix, partly from the splendour of the pure gold, partly from the singular brilliancy of the enamel. The figure in ivory of our Saviour is altogether conventional in treatment, severe also and archaic in style. There is, however, not only dignity in the disposition of the body and limbs but tenderness in the drooping head. The arms (separate pieces) are widely extended, and the feet rest divided on a small table to support them. A crown of thorns is round the head, and the hair is carefully divided into numerous plaits which fall behind and over the shoulders. The clothing is fastened with a broad girdle round the waist and falls below the knees. The ivory is walrus ivory.

The cross itself, an inch and a half broad and seven and a half in height, is covered with thin plates of gold of great purity. The flat gold is again covered by a granulated line, forming a scroll decoration which rolls over the whole surface. Over the head of the figure is the title IHS NAZARENVS; and at the four extremities of the cross are roundels containing the evangelistic symbols in very brilliant *cloisonné* enamel. The dividing lines of gold are very thin ; and the effect of each is so bright and full in colour as to have the appearance of *pietra dura* work. The gold on the reverse is thin and soft, in consequence of which the decoration has been much injured. The lamb and the four evangelistic symbols in roundels are to be dimly discerned amongst the folds and wrinkles into which the metal has been rubbed.

This beautiful crucifix was obtained from the Soltikoff collection, when sold in 1862 ; and is Byzantine work, probably of the tenth century. Goldsmiths' work of that famous school, which may be said to have begun in the fourth century and lasted until the eleventh, is excessively rare. Compared with the art of classic Rome that of Byzantium was almost barbarous. Occasionally we can find examples (like the present) combining work in ivory, gold, and enamel, in which the designs are not wanting either in grace or dignity. These, however, are exceptions. Constantinople inherited what was left of Roman art, but used her inheritance only as a sort of representation of older and better forms. Byzantine traditions became fixed in centuries later than the ninth, and modern workmen in Greece, Russia, and Constantinople still cling to and retain them. The fine enamels of the best Byzantine period were, like those at the extremities of this cross, always *cloisonné*; not like those of France and Cologne in later times, *champlevé*.

Bought for 145*l.*

COFFER OR RELIQUARY   WOOD, CARVED, PAINTED, AND GILT   BYZANTINE 12TH OR 13TH CENT.

4 6IN x 3 IN W8   S K M (N°54-54)   W™ CATLEY RECIT

COFFER.

WOOD; CARVED, PAINTED, AND GILT.

No. 582—1854.

THIS box or coffer, of a date probably as early as the twelfth century, is a rare and good example of Rhenish-Byzantine work. Few such exist which are carved in wood : in metal or ivory or bone they are more often met with. The style of that age is peculiarly characteristic ; rude, but full of force and dignity. Grotesque animals only and foliated ornaments form the decorations of this casket. In other examples the same ornaments are found with human figures, or dogs, stags, and wild beasts. However twisted and wound together the different convolutions which are formed might (at first sight) seem to be, a little examination will show that they are symmetrically arranged and that every winding has been carefully designed with a very decided intention. The decorations may appear to be conventional but they are really made up of individual parts, separately thought out and carried to a distinct end. The style gradually died out soon after the beginning of the thirteenth century.

The front panel is filled with four figures of fabulous animals, griffins, &c.: at the two ends there are merely knobs. The cover, pyramidal in shape with a flat top, is divided into five panels. These also are decorated with grotesque beasts, and the intermediate spaces filled with the usual foliated ornamentation. On the back are interlaced chequers, a quatrefoil in relief filling each square space. The bottom is also lined out into four square panels, with a light line ornament incised. There are remains of colour and gilding on the animals and foliated decorations.

The coffer is six inches and a half in height, and about thirteen inches in length.

Bought for 20*l.*

PAIR OF BRONZE SNUFFERS. ITALIAN CINQUE CENTO. — 8⅝ IN.
(HERNAL OIL)   S.K.M. (№ 2091)   W. WISE FEC T.

195

SNUFFERS.

BRONZE.

No. 2081—1855.

A FAIR example of careful art decoration applied to common things in daily use. The snuffers are Italian, and of a time when the pupils of Donatello himself were working in bronze: at the beginning or the middle of the sixteenth century.

The top of the box has in the centre a female head, winged and with a helmet; on either side is a terminal figure of a woman. Below the head is a grotesque mask, and above it the profile apparently of a Roman emperor in a medallion; the whole decoration arranged under a trefoil arch. Each handle finishes with a coil like a snake's; and the stems are richly ornamented with terminal figures standing upon pedestals, and these, again, are divided into small panels.

The snuffers were in the Bernal collection; dispersed in 1855.

Bought for 1l. 3s.

MIRROR CASE.

IVORY.

No. 210—1865.

I N shape this mirror case is similar to the mirror case which has been
engraved and described in plate six. It is also of the same date, about
1270, and may with equal justice be attributed to an English artist,
although ivories of this class and style have for a long time been, too
hastily perhaps, given to French sculptors. One remark cannot be dis-
puted : that there are numerous ivory carvings existing, of the fourteenth
and fifteenth centuries, which it is quite impossible to refer with absolute
certainty either to the English or the French school. In some instances
we have a guide if we can trace their pedigree, or know from whence they
were obtained ; about others we may have a known history. But where
these evidences fail, we must be content to remain in doubt.

This mirror case is quite as charming in design and as good in
execution as the other which has been already selected ; in fact, being
divided into two compartments, there is more variety in the subjects ; and
the decoration of the double series of arcades gives a remarkable richness
to the whole composition.

But it is not so easy to explain the subject, which has probably been
taken from some romance. The siege of the Castle of Love almost explained itself; but here we have what seems to be a little history of a
long courtship, beginning from the left of the lower compartment.

In this compartment, upon the left, a lady seems to be receiving a
present of a dog from a gentleman to whom she is talking in the centre,
and again receives him in the next division, accepting (as it were) his
proffered homage, clasped hands placed within her own. These six, or
the pair repeated twice, stand under a rich arcade of six cusped arches
with bold crockets. They are in a garden in which are shown flowering
shrubs.

In the upper compartment we find seven figures under a canopy of
three divisions, of which the middle is as large as the other two together.

I. 96

Whether the side arches give again the same pair still continuing their courtship is by no means clear; but the centre group appears to represent the happy conclusion of the whole affair, in the presence of a crowned personage before whom the lady and the gentleman kneel, one upon each side.

Another explanation may be given of this mirror case; that the persons shown are independent of each other, and are merely friends in the room of a palace, or walking together in a garden. But the group of three under the large arch certainly seems to allude to some tale or passage from a romance.

The inside border of the outer circle is further decorated with a number of small roses; and outside are four crawling dragons. These last served probably the more easily to open the mirror case, of which the ivory which exists simply formed the cover.

Ivory mirror cases of the middle ages, no less than caskets or writing-tablets or other ornamental objects of small size, are of great importance and interest because they supply contemporary evidence of costume and armour, sometimes also of domestic manners and customs. In this respect they are records as valuable as illuminations in manuscripts. They show us not only scenes from the favourite poems and stories of the time, but people " in their habits as they lived," sometimes playing at chess or draughts, or other games; sometimes riding, or hawking, or hunting; sometimes dancing; sometimes, as in this mirror case, in gardens with dogs and birds. Nor is the subject always limited to secular matters : scripture histories are often carved. Upon mirror cases, combs, or other toilet articles, of these stories from the Bible the message from David to Bathsheba is the most frequent.

This mirror case measures nearly six inches in diameter.

Bought for 75*l.*